THE
TAP DRESSERS
A Celebration

A PERSONAL ACCOUNT
OF A WELLDRESSING VILLAGE

by

Norman Wilson

COUNTRY BOOKS

Published by Country Books
Courtyard Cottage, Little Longstone, Bakewell, Derbyshire DE45 1NN

ISBN 1 898941 47 5

ACKNOWLEDGEMENTS

My thanks to Bridget for her patient expertise.
Also to A. Brassington, D. Brown, M. Fell, F. W. Shimwell, S. Shimwell
and R. Wilson for kindly providing the photographs.

A Dedication

Dedication indeed. It is a word that, with a different shade of meaning from that intended here, could as aptly decorate the title were not *celebration* a more compelling motif for what is to follow. Dedication of tribute and spirit must have been the essence of welldressing since it first began – and no other epithet so completely serves the cause. But *Celebration* must prevail for, as the rest of the Christian world is about to mark the Millennium, so the welldressers of Youlgrave have their own special event to commemorate.

Welldressers are not merely *rehearsing* an ancient custom: it is a part of them. Here there are craftsmen whose personal commitment covers a large part of this century and whose memory by association reaches well into the last. But it is among the designers that we find this commitment most conspicuously demonstrated. Paragons there are aplenty, and it casts no reflection on the rest of them when I mention three in special tribute.

Frederick W. Shimwell

Margaret Fell

James Shimwell

3

This year, 1999, both Fred and Margaret completed 50 continuous years as designers, a staggering achievement for them individually, a remarkable record for the village and a focus for the gratitude of all who have come, year on year, to admire their work. Fred has taken his metaphorical gold watch this year; Margaret punctiliously awaits the Millennium.

They began designing together at Bank Top in 1949, Fred as designer of the picture and in overall charge of the *Tap*, leaving Margaret to execute the border. The next year, 1950, she accepted an invitation to take charge of the postwar restoration of Coldwell, while Fred continued in sole charge at Bank Top. So, this year, he quite rightly claimed the record of having designed the same *tap* for fifty years, whereas Margaret prefers to defer her own jubilee to the fifty years she will have been in charge at Coldwell. Since neither cares for fuss, this tribute given in admiration of their achievement may well provide as much public acknowledgement as either is prepared to tolerate.

Would I could be so light-hearted about the third member of this distinguished and dedicated group. Sadly, Jim designed his last welldressing in 1997. In the late morning of Saturday, 22nd June, he died as he had lived, in the service of welldressing. As ever, he had checked round the five *taps* to ensure that all was ready for the Blessing of the Wells. He had photographed the screens for the records and was returning home – healthy and active in middle age so it seemed – when he collapsed and died.

So in this dedication I must sadly couple celebration with valediction. Jim was the guardian of the Youlgrave tradition and its integrity, our ethical conscience. He was the Secretary who almost single-handedly for forty years provided the organisation without which his fellow artists would have had no canvas.

Perhaps he provided the inspiration – most certainly the encouragement – for this book, earlier parts of which were written to reflect his ongoing influence. Should I, then, amend them accordingly? I think not: his death diminishes neither the significance nor the vitality of what he had to say to us and, in leaving things as we wish they could still be, I hope none will take it amiss.

Norman Wilson
Youlgrave
December 1999

PREFACE

We welldressers on the whole are not given to introspection. Our congregations are entirely practical and we go about what is essentially a pleasant annual chore without dwelling too much on the meaning of life and our place in the universe. At least we know what we are doing even though we may not be entirely sure why we are doing it. Such explanations as may be thought necessary are generally left to the cognoscenti. So why do I, a welldressing dogsbody, seek to add yet another publication to an already comprehensive list? Do we really need another book about welldressing?

Perhaps not, but another book about *welldressing* is not what this is meant to be. It is a subjective account of a village that happens to dress its wells – or more accurately its *tapspots*. It is about the whys and wherefores, above all about the people the visitors rarely see – the designers and dressers and the community they serve. Its motive lies in awareness that we have something very special to celebrate, a remarkable occasion that we should be proud to share. To have one designer with a record of fifty years' outstanding experience must be rare in welldressing circles; to have two is surely unique.

There is another reason we may be less eager to acknowledge: Youlgrave welldressers make poor hosts. If it may seem that once the screens are up and *blessed* we go home and forget about them and our guests for the next six days, the impression is not without foundation. We can but plead guilty, but in mitigation, it must be remembered in our favour that the ephemeral glory of a welldressing is at its brief peak when the last petal goes into the clay on Friday night/Saturday morning, from there on it is all down hill. If backs are turned; it is from the inexorable decline of the screens and not from our welcome visitors. We knock off on Saturday thinking our work to be done for another year, but of course it isn't.

It took an incident a few years ago to reveal the truth of it to me. Busy setting up the public address system prior to the Blessing of the Wells at Holywell, I was taken for an *official* and, in responding to a question from a visitor in the gathering congregation, found myself with an instant audience. There I was, talking to... well, not the casual sightseers I had always supposed them to be, lured by another folksy tourist spectacle to fill a summer Saturday afternoon... I was talking to *connoisseurs* whose interest ran deeeper than mere visual curiosity. We who live here take welldressing for what it is – an integral part of the community, as firmly embedded in past and present as the gravestones in the churchyard and as relevant to village history as the fabric of the buildings. It was a truth that, had we thought about it at all, we would expect to elude our passing visitors. Not so: my erstwhile audience had clearly perceived it. Their questions were as much about the community as the welldressings it produced and it was we who had failed, in all modesty, to discern it. It is a persistent misunderstanding. The visitors have come to see the welldressings; why should they be interested in us, the welldressers, in who we are, what we are and why. We do not advertise, we do not seek converts, we do not even associate with other welldressers. To all intents and purposes, Youlgrave welldressings could be the work of elves.

This, then, aspires not to be another exposition of welldressing so much as the depiction of a village that happens to dress its former public tapspots. It is about a welldressing *community*

7

– as opposed to a welldressing *location*. Yet, for all its narrow focus, I hope there will be enough of general interest to satisfy the curiosity of that discerning visitor, wherever he may be, who finds a mere passing glimpse of welldressing inadequate and aspires to learn more. It will be of little interest to the tripper who likes to *do the welldressing tour* from the seat of a bus, nor will it appeal much to the expert who declares *"see one and you've seen the lot"*. It is as much about people as the art they employ.

But – a word of caution – I am not to be trusted too far. The subjective memory allows youthful impressions to masquerade as facts, even when the truth emerges. This is the inherent risk in writing about a village that has always been one's *home*, but perhaps the reader will allow that sentimental notions and impressions, whether one's own or handed down, are the yeast without which any subjective account is in danger of falling flat. Why be browbeaten by the truth when it serves only to banish cherished illusions ?

I have long been old enough to know better, but my memory cleaves to the myth of one boyhood village experience in the same way that Santa Claus was long given the benefit of doubt. The scene is Stores Hill (between the Fountain and Holywell Lane) where I stood as a boy to watch the Welldressing Procession many years ago. In those days there was a close association with the Ancient Order of Foresters who, for historical reasons, held their club feast in the Bulls Head Hotel at Midsummer prior to heading the joint parade through the main street. I can clearly see it now, as it was – or as it is watermarked in my memory. At the head of the parade moving towards me was the huge banner of the Lodge borne by two mightily-striving standard-bearers, at once sweating in the June sun and staggering this way and that across the street as they fought against the buffeting wind. It is an heroic memory, which is somehow bracketed in my mind with a contemporary recollection of a frosty morning in Bakewell Square when, with a clamour of sudden excitement, a timber-laden

8

drug[1] appeared drawn by a team of six mighty shires, steam jetting from their nostrils and sparks flying from their hooves as the whips cracked over their flanks. I can easily ascribe to both memories the same noble vision, but alas, the comparison is a childish illusion. There was no wind, no breeze at all, as I watched on that Midsummer day. If, indeed, one of the four elements was to blame for the loss of the standard-bearers' equilibrium, it was certainly not air or even earth and fire (except in the metaphorical sense): it had to be water – water that steeped the hops that filled the vats to brew the beer that went to the legs of the Foresters. Part of growing up was to learn that, for those worldly enough to recognise the symptoms, it was – and still is – a village joke.

There may be other illusions I still unwittingly nurture and, more culpable still, am not of a mind to discard in the cause of scholarly research. My impressions are genuine, their provenance may be less reliable. Does it matter if I accidently tell an apochryphal story or repeat a legend? Youlgrave, to be sure, has more than its share of both, and as long as everyone knows...

---

[1] heavy dray used for carting stone blocks and timber

Chapter 1

ROOTS

Welldressing notwithstanding, perhaps the most unusual thing about the village where I belong is that nobody knows how to spell it. Should it be *Youlgrave* or *Youlgreave*? It is a question that perplexes most visitors – and not a few residents – so perhaps it is as well that they are not confronted with the additional thirty-three alternatives that, according to the local historian J.W. Shimwell, have been recorded since it first appeared as *Giolgrave* in the Domesday Survey. The good news is that they are all redundant and, as to the two that remain, there are authoritative sources for using either. *Youlgrave* is my choice but I am not prepared to go to the stake for it.

So – and this must be popular question number two – with so many names to choose from, why does everybody call it *Pommy*? To that there is no answer.

In the beginning... any account of a custom so unusual as well-dressing ought logically to begin with a description of what it is, but on the assumption that most people interested enough to have got this far will have already seen at least one example, I will save the technical details for later. This is an account, as promised, of a village community and why, each year, it practises an art-form as fragile and transient as pavement artistry without the obvious reason for doing it. There is no perceivable reason why Youlgrave should be a traditional welldressing village: we can, at best, speculate from the standpoint of history and social experience why it has survived as such.

The history of Youlgrave, in common with the rest of the district, is what historians call *shrouded*, the principal reason being that the literati were not anxious to come here. Daniel Defoe, who did, lingered long enough to condemn the orefield and its inhabitants as a kind of Devil's Island best avoided by respectable people with a choice in the matter. Some sketchy reference is made in various County publications and while more information can be gleaned from topic-related sources, there was little written prior to this century that featured the village people and how they lived. Like most rural communities of its kind, a great deal was handed down by word of mouth from one generation to the next, but fact and fable come this way with equal credence and, in any case, the art of discourse has been going out of fashion.

There are two latter-day publications available to anyone sufficiently interested to track them down. A former vicar, the Reverend W. Parker Stamper, gave us *Youlgrave, A Derbyshire Village*, in 1901, having promised to *"purpose, during this season of most inclement weather, devoting some of my spare time in searching for a more clear history of the past than has already come to light"*. Although, understandably, it seems to be written from the perspective of the church vestry in a romantic style that occasionally forgoes mundane fact, it is redolent of a community on the threshold of a century of dramatic change. Thirty years later, the ladies of the Women's Institute produced a publication called *Some Account of Youlgrave, Middleton & Alport*. Though clearly influenced by Miss Melland's[1] broad erudition in the historical context, it stands as a notable

---

[1] Village librarian and the last of a benevolent and influential family of Middleton and Youlgrave

achievement for so small an Institute. As to the placename, they *"can give only probabilities"* and lay claim to only nineteen alternatives. So, if we are to rely on speculation, Mr. Shimwell himself has an attractive contribution to make:

> *"...by reference to a dictionary of the old English language.* **Geolu** *was the old English word for yellow and* **graefe** *can be variously translated as a pit, trench or grave, or a grove of trees.*
>
> *"The origins are obscure and several theories have been put forward. One theory suggests that the first part of the name is derived from the personal name of a local dignitary, Geola or Iola, and that the settlement was his entrenched house. A more satisfactory explanation may be developed. In Derbyshire, the lead mines were for centuries referred to as groves or grooves and, thus, it seems probable that the original name of Youlgrave can be translated as 'yellow mine'. To the geologist, Youlgrave is recognised as the centre of a zone in which the mineral barytes is associated with the lead in the veins. The mineral is also known as caulk and produces a characteristic yellow-brown staining on the soil, which could account for the origin of the* **geolu** *element in the village name."*

Local people, who not all that long ago spoke a dialect as rich as it was incomprehensible to anyone south of the Trent, pronounced it *Yo-gree* – or, less respectfully, *Pommy*. How the village came by the nickname is, again, a matter for speculation, although most people agree it has something to do with the old village band. Old-fashioned inter-village one-upmanship may be to blame.

Rivalry... it must be noted, was endemic between villages and anyone caught off his own ground could expect to be taunted – mostly, but not always – in good humour. There were rituals to be observed, one of which was reserved for the newcomer. *Aye*, the greeting would go, *that's wheer they...* "they" being the rival villagers identified with the particular example of collective idiocy reserved for them. Bonsall was the place where they cut the cow's head off to get it out of the gate. Tideswell was where they put wire-netting over the cabbages to keep the frost out. Youlgrave was where they put the pig on the wall to listen to the band. It is a ritual insult with which an eskimo might still be teased if he came to live here.

"Pom – pom" was said to be the prevailing sound of the band in its formative years,[2] so Pommyites we became and Pommyites we remain to anyone born within a day's walking distance of the parish – mildly derisory in the fashion that lesser beings mock their betters – just a part of the good-natured rivalry that permeated all but more serious encounters such as sport and courting – in that order.

... and harmony. There was no rivalry in the business of welldressing for the simple reason that there was no other village handy enough to be rivals with. Mr. Stamper, whose matters-of-fact it has to be said sometimes contained a grain of fiction, names only three other locations, Tissington, Buxton, and Wirksworth,[3] and they, being outside the banter-zone, would have been correspondingly beyond notice.

So, unlike the dubious welcome extended to, say, a rival football team, the annual welldressing festival was forever a model of cordiality and good grace. People from other villages would come in their Sunday-best, a mark of respect and accord, in return for which they would be granted the status of authenticated critics. Friends would visit friends and dispersed families would briefly foregather. It was a time of renewed loyalties and family commitment, the essence of which is still a feature of the Youlgrave festival today.

---

[2] mid 1870s

[3] I was reliably told at first-hand that the four welldressing locations at the turn of the century were Barlow, Tissington, Wirksworth and Youlgrave, but knowing how vehemently challenged the list may be, I stand to be corrected

Leadmining... A vital ingredient of welldressing was, and must still be, a strong community spirit. Anyone coming from the coalfield on the eastern side of the County should not be surprised to recognise, in Youlgrave, a community as closely-bonded as the mining village he has left behind. Believe it or not, this, too, is a mining village both in history and character and, while there is little evidence to show for it now, the industry has left its presence in the folk-memory, in the recollections of its elderly residents, in its idiom, its vocabulary,[4] and its shared values. To be sure, it was leadmining and not coalmining that shaped its character, but the essential influences were the same: the imperative of working together without discord, awareness of mutual interest in the face of hardship and hazard and the sanctity of what little leisure accrued. These were the constraints that tempered the social and religious life of the village.

Perhaps more than any other, the influence of leadmining shaped the language and habits of our forebears. But it was water that shaped their fortunes. Over the centuries the economy, vitality and size of the village varied indirectly with the level of water in the mines – a predicament, indeed, for the welldressing miner who, having given thanks for the gift of water, went to bed praying for less of it at work.

Although the craft of mining prevailed for another thirty years in the winning of associated vein minerals, leadmining in the parish ended in 1932 when an explosion in the last active mine, Shining Gutter, took the lives of five miners and suffocated three others who tried to rescue them. It is a melancholy thought that evidence of the once-staple industry that so influenced our language and customs – yes, even our supersti-

---

4 the wooden channel that drained the workface was called a launder. Ask any Youlgravian what collects the water from a roof and he is unlikely to say 'a gutter', he will call it a **launder**, ask him what gathers surface water from the highway and he will call it a **sough** because that was the adit that drained the orefield

14

tions – is now most readily found in the churchyard.

What influence, if any, leadmining had on the form and persistence of welldressing belongs in the realm of conjecture; suffice it for now to say that I am not numbered amongst the popular theorists who reckon it all began in one particular village and the rest copied what looked like a good idea.

... and quarrying... Though you now have to search for the remains of Youlgrave's first extractive industry, there is no lack of evidence of its second. It is sufficient to stand on the street and look around. The same limestone bedrock through which the miners tunnelled for their galena was quarried within the parish to build their houses and surface the highways. All the houses in the conservation area are built in limestone – the most readily available material – while the quoins and dressed surrounds suggest there was a source of gritstone not far away. The assumption is justified. For centuries men trudged daily across the fields to Harthill and beyond to win and shape the gritstone for countless purposes at home and abroad: ashlar for prestigious buildings, massive blocks for reservoir and railway construction, grindstones and filestones for Sheffield, pulpstones for Scandinavia, drinking troughs, garden ornaments and building stone. Wet or fine, daylight and dark, they trod the paths that are now the jealously-guarded province of ramblers and hikers.

Hard and hazardous though it undoubtedly was, most people will now see quarrying as a good career move from tunnelling underground, and in all but one important respect it probably was. The exception, paradoxically, is that which may seem to be its redeeming feature: it was open to the fresh air and this had its serious downside. When the frost was in the stone it was unworkable, so the quarryman stayed at home without wages while his mining neighbour enjoyed the benefit of a near-constant working environment and an uninterrupted income throughout the year. The quarryman and his family could be destitute for weeks at a time which, with nothing put by, could have meant starvation. There were good reasons why it never did: an instinctive understanding that those who had shared with those who had not[5], a philosophy reinforced in substance by the Youlgrave Stores[6] (a provident and assured defence against the vicissitudes of winter) and the friendly societies that consolidated the strong spirit of interdependence and mutual concern. It is no coincidence that the latter share with the Waterworks Committee the credit for sustaining the welldressing custom in Youlgrave when other villages may have fallen by the wayside.

*   *   *   *   *   *

Limestone quarrying still features prominently in the local economy. Machines have largely removed the relentless drudgery, but machines have no characters to enhearten the daily round. It is a quirk of nature that the more rigorous a society the more animated it seemed, the more individuality asserted itself and the more fondly we reflect on its merits.

Time back, there were certain unattached men who, hard-working and reliable as a rule, would take time off from work on impulse (I suppose when the drudgery got too irksome), leave home and *sleep rough* for days at a time. They were either

---

[5] A quaint variety of the principle was the convention of *the latchlifter*, a convention by which a man would not be denied the means to drown his sorrows at a time when he was most in need. The latchlifter was the price of the first jar of ale – or more specifically, of acquiring the pot it came in, which could then be maintained at "a convenient depth" for the rest of the evening as more affluent companions topped it up at regular intervals.

[6] The Youlgrave Stores, an early version (1870) of the C.W.S., part of which it later became, enabled families to put a little by in prosperous seasons and to obtain goods on credit to see them through the troughs. Sadly, it is now defunct and its last premises are the Youth Hostel, but it is still redolent of the mahogany fittings, the bacon slicer and the groceries in which we older residents remember it with affection.

16

gregarious or solitary. The former spent their available cash (or that of some chance companion) on an extended pub-crawl; the latter would roam the neighbourhood, content with their own thoughts and company, perhaps building up a wall here and there or performing some other minor public service as a backdrop to their ruminations. One such was Isaac G. – not his real name, but near enough – who worked at Shining Bank Quarry when it was a much smaller concern. He was known amongst his workmates for his unhurried thought processes.

One day, the topic of discussion over their mid-day sand-wiches was a legal execution that had taken place that morning in Strangeways gaol. The cabin-talk moved on from the particular circumstances of the case to a debate involving the morality of capital punishment, then to methods more accept-able than hanging. Throughout it all Isaac sat in thoughtful silence, making no contribution of his own. As the end of breaktime drew nigh, discussion had rolled on to the question of resurrection, life after death and, finally, to the prospect of re-incarnation. Isaac's silence was no longer acceptable. *"What do you think Isaac?"*, someone eventually asked. Isaac gazed ahead, clearly pondering the issue, while his workmates hung on his answer. *"Do, you believe in re-incarnation?"* At last Isaac drew breath to answer: *"No"*, he said vehemently, *"Ah think they should hang the b*****s".*

*   *   *   *   *   *

In the beginning... of course, none of these village characteris-tics and influences would have had any relevance to the cus-tom of welldressing had it not existed in the first place. Yes, they feature as recognisable reasons why it should flourish here; they throw no light on the origins for any record of which we will search in vain. Conjecture is all we have. Or do we have some atavistic folk memory lurking at the back of our consciousness. Perhaps a short journey into history will serve to quicken it.

Within the eastern confines of Youlgrave parish is a hamlet steeped in history. Alport now shows little of its past, but here was once a ford on the Manchester to Derby road, a lead smelter[7] the ruins of which may still be seen and the Alport Mining Company, said in its day to be one of the largest producers of lead in Europe. There is an outcrop of tufa limestone from where John Wesley is said to have preached a sermon. Across the road is Haddon Fields Farmhouse, once the family home of J.P. Joule, the scientist who gave his name to a unit of energy. On the cartshed gable there used to be a painted sign so old that the lettering had become embossed by the weather. It notified the world that *All vagrants found lodging, strolling or begging within this parish will be taken up and dealt with as the law directs.* It is gone now, hopefully for preservation, and a replica put in its place, though no doubt the sentiment lingers on. Preserved too, at least in the writer's memory. is the jingle:

Over Haddon, Nether Haddon, Haddon-on-the-Hill
And if you go to Alport, you'll find a paper mill

Not any longer. The picturesque old building by the stream that causes people to linger in admiration on the bridge is an old cornmill; all traces of the paper mill were obliterated long ago.

But we are not here to visit the pages of recorded history. Here where the waters of the Lathkill rush tumbling to join the Bradford is a good place to begin a short journey into the realm of fancy. Imagine this confluence before – long before – the mills and the mines, when there were no buildings to be seen, not even the ancient *Monks Hall* that stands on the edge of the stream, and where there was no human excrescence to invade the grotto-like magic of the dell. Surely, it would be in such a place as this that the ancient pantheists would come

---

[7] the short stretch of road immediately to the east is still known locally as *Cupulow* (i.e. Cupola)

with their floral offerings or, as travellers fording the stream, pause for a blessing on their journey. Alport has no welldressing of its own, but who knows. might it not be here that the strands of tradition begin?

The narrow, unclassified lane from Alport to Elton is a thoroughfare of great antiquity. Once over the bridge we are in the scattered parish of Harthill, climbing up through the last of the limestone to the gritstone ridge above. The grey walls change to a warmer brown and the air is filled with the earthy aroma of acid-loving vegetation; springs well from the hillside. Three hundred yards further along and one hundred and forty feet higher, we are suddenly surrounded by 5,000 years of human continuity. To our left, the four standing stones (orthostats) that survive from the original Nine Stone Close are a Neolithic/Bronze Age circle, the setting for arcane events and superstitions that have persisted in folklore right into this century. To our right, Castle Ring is the earthworks of an Iron Age fort. Ahead, the foreground is dominated by the twin-chimneyed pile of Robin Hood's Stride behind which lie the remains of a Romano-British village. Finally, sheltering in the lee of Cratcliffe Rocks where the ancient highway the Portway dips down toward Dudwood, is our link with Christianity: the Hermits Cave, home of a Mediaeval anchorite who, between seeking gifts and alms from superstitious travellers, carved in the rock wall of his home the evidence of his faith – a crucifix. So in the space of a few score acres do we span the centuries from pagan to Christian. Although in no other respect is this historical continuity so clearly a feature of the Youlgrave locality, the parish is surrounded by evidence – Arbor Low, Bee Low, Benty Grange – of a community rooted in prehistory. It is, then, perhaps not too much of a conjecture to presume that the same continuum is to be found in its ancient customs.

Floralia, and the like ... There is ample evidence that the prehistoric practice of decking the wells and watercourses with floral tributes to a variety of gods was widespread throughout

Europe. It is also fairly well-established that this is one of the customs where the early Christians thought it prudent to adapt a heathen practice rather than try and put a stop to it. Later generations were less tolerantly indulged. There were times of ascetic rigour when celebration was severely discouraged and all but the most tenacious customs ceased to be observed. Nowhere, it should be noted, was superstition more indelibly rooted than in the vein mineral mines of Cornwall, Cumberland and Derbyshire.

Few people now doubt that welldressing has its origins in prehistoric rites. What finds a good deal less agreement are the answers to these questions: *Why is it predominantly in the Derbyshire Dales that adorning the springs has persisted?* and *How did it become the art-form that it is?* The plain fact is that one guess is as good as another and, on the strict understanding that guessing is what we're about, I can only offer my own pet theory.

In recent times the village of Ashford-in-the-Water has established a form of twinning with a town in Italy called Aquapendente. The bond between them is a welldressing tradition that is, at once, strikingly similar and strikingly different. The welldressers of Aquapendente do not create their screens by pressing flower petals into beds of clay. They select foliage – a leaf, say – for its precise colour, then cut it to shape before sticking it with adhesive to a large, flat, backing board. Thus, leaf by leaf, an imposing picture is built up – a welldressing in appearance if not in technique. Therein lies the food for speculation.

The ancient Roman festival of Floralia was dedicated to the spirits of streams and fountains. The Romans were drawn here to exploit the lead veins and relax in the thermal springs of what is now largely West Derbyshire. Could it be that they introduced an Italian refinement to the established local custom? and could it be that welldressing and leadmining are inextricably linked after all?

Pure imagination, of course, with no shred of evidence to support it, but we all need our *Roots*..

Above: *Monks Hall from the old footbridge crossing the Lathkill. Beyond the house, the river plunges down a cascade to join the Bradford 75 yards upstream of this point.*

Below: *Robin Hood's Stride seen through the orthostats. It was earlier named* Mock Beggars Hall *because mendicant travellers coming across the White Peak and seeing the pile from afar, took it to be a great hall where they could expect food and lodging for the night, only to discover its true nature on arrival. The Portway runs across the foreground and is about to dip down towards Dudwood.*

21

The Hermit's Cave at Cratcliffe Rocks. This shallow recess at the base of the rock, screened by an ancient yew tree, is now protected by iron railings to prevent vandals chipping off pieces of the crucifix for souvenirs.

Chapter 2

TAPSPOTS

The mechanics of a welldressing are simple. A collection of interlocking boards are faced with clay into which decorative vegetation is pressed to form a pattern or picture. The screen is then raised to public view at a specific point in the village street so that people may come to see it. This laconic description invites a whole series of associated questions which are neither simple nor easy to answer coherently. *Who makes it? Why? What is it for? Why is it there?* If only these issues and a few more like them could be so tidily compartmented! Trying to think in straight lines about a welldressing village is like gathering sheep: the topics are either inextricably huddled or bolting off on their own.

Since welldressing is a thanksgiving for water, water is where we should begin and, contrary to all expectation, wells are not where it will be found in Youlgrave. There are no wells, which will come as little surprise to the visitors I see peering round the back of screens like pilgrims at Lourdes. They are 200 years too late and it must be very disappointing for them to have their expectations raised by romantic-sounding names like *Coldwell* and *Holywell* only to have them dashed on learning these are nothing more than street names. We dress *Taps*, which years ago were prosaically known as *Top Tap, Middle*

Tap, and so on, a style of identification that lingers in the language of the older residents. And to head off anyone who might be exposed to further disappointment, I have to confess there are no taps either – only tapspots.

1829 and all that ... Youlgrave did once have its public wells and it could be that the stand taps that replaced them were positioned close by the former sites so as to cause minimum disruption to established habits. The wells were abandoned early in the 19th Century when the installation of drainage culverts was thought to be a potential source of pollution. Residents without an alternative private supply had to carry water in buckets from the River Bradford, a major daily chore that must have impelled the remarkable community project that was to follow. In the centre of the village, where the village cross once stood[1], there stands a large stone cistern dated 1829. It commemorates the completion of a scheme to pipe water from a gritstone spring at Mawstone (*Mall Stone*) Farm, a distance of 1100 yards, at a cost of £252.13.10½ which was met from public subscription.[2]

The water was first supplied direct from the spring to this central point by gravity and, as the surplus *head* was dissipated by an upward spout, it became known as *The Fountain*. A supply pipe – still visible – was closed by a locked faucet and opened at set times daily by the water keeper to allow subscribers to fill their buckets. And as freely as the water ran the on-site village gossip was sure to match it.

We who take an effortless supply of water for granted can hardly imagine what a boon it must have been. Who knows, it may have inspired a collective sense of gratitude so enduring

---

[1] now to be seen on the north side of the churchyard

[2] Set in the floor of the south aisle of the parish church is a stone plaque inscribed, simply, *HB*. It is a very modest memorial to a remarkable woman. Hannah Bowman, a gentlewoman from an old Youlgrave family, who provided the inspiration and the leadership to accomplish this major enterprise.

that ... no, we cannot have it said that Youlgrave celebrates an annual *Thanksgiving For Not Having to Carry Water From the River.* The price of this privilege, two buckets of water and access to the 19th Century version of *Internet*, was sixpence (2½p) per annum.

The inauguration was marked by celebrations, the more edifying of which were happily recorded in a newsheet – *happily* because it mentions *a special welldressing* and that provides us with the earliest written evidence of the custom in Youlgrave. It does not, as some are prone to claim, indicate the date when the custom began. Could it not be that this one-off, grand occasion turned the spotlight on an already-established tradition that has existed for a good deal more than 170 years. But I won't go into it now[3], other than to enquire: *if it were not an established, familiar custom, why no mention of the experts who came to do it?*

Youlgrave has kept its own private water supply ever since, somehow slipping the net of amalgamations elsewhere, but before readers rush off to fill their containers with free spring water that costs money in supermarkets, I have to confess that this vision of a sparkling elixir is a little out-of-date. The pristine quality of which we were once so proud – even boastful – has succumbed to the squeamishness of E.C. dictates and is *treated.* That is not all. The relentless increase in village water consumption[4], coupled with national drought, has forced the Youlgrave Waterworks to look for an ancillary source of supply, and where else have they found it but in the old Shining Gutter leadmine, the last of the industry for which an abundance of water had been a constant bane. There is food for thought.

3 There is no need. J.W. & D.W. Shimwell produced a thoroughly researched history in 1974, extracts from which I am privileged to append.

4 Youlgrave Waterworks Committee confessed itself inundated (if that can be the right word) by 1970s and called on a supplier for new developments. As well as disposing of the village sewage, this supplier discreetly stands by to help out should the need arise.

Forty years after its inauguration the system was in need of major refurbishment, so in 1869 the mains were relaid by an arrangement that now seems quaint but which was a familiar means of maintaining the roads in those days. Each adult male in the parish gave either his labour or a cash contribution in kind. The system became even more user-friendly by the installation of a service main throughout the village to supply a series of tapspots much closer to home. The five serving the main street were selected for *tapdressing* and so they have remained in spirit if not precisely in position ever since. If, as seems probable, there were multiple welldressings before this time, nobody can say where they were, but it may not be stretching the imagination too far to suppose the tapspots – and, *per se*, the welldressing screens – were located to serve a pattern of neighbourhood focal points established by the old wells. What is known for sure is that these have been the welldressing sites, with minor variations and interruptions, for as long as anyone can say.

Teams ... Equally immutable are the teams that have dressed them. The number of taps dressed is always five. It is a fixed number, each with its own designer and each with its own band of workers who are so firmly *hefted* onto their workstation that transfer and interchange between *taps* is virtually unknown. This loyalty is established on arrival in the village – which is at birth for the majority – and it is not unknown for married couples to part company for an evening's welldressing because their dedication to separate taps pre-dates their dedication to each other. Each team operates autonomously under its designer, who selects the subject, draws the design and templates, prepares the equipment, arranges and directs the dressing and organises the supply of natural materials. A formidable responsibility it may seem, but the teams are so well-established that delegation is virtually self-generating.

The Youlgrave designers, through their technical competence, their consistency, their experience and their leadership, have brought welldressing, year on year, to artistic levels rarely matched elsewhere. Moreover, no other village has brought so much influence to bear on the wider welldressing scene through its designers acting in a private capacity. It is recognisable in the common strand of form and technique that students of the art will perceive as the *Youlgrave influence* in several other villages.

By 1997, four of Youlgrave's five designers had 147 years service between them so it is easy to mistake the phenomenon for the norm and overlook the coherence of the teams. There have been times in the past when a particular *tap* (as distinct from the whole festival) has failed to be dressed. The explanation may lie in a variety of reasons, favourite of which might be thought to be for want of a designer. The evidence from 1928 suggests otherwise. That year, G.W. Gimber, the local headmaster, designed all five taps and five very commendable welldressings were produced[5]. By no stretch of the imagination could he have simultaneously supervised five screens as closely as we are now used to: it serves to illustrate how self-sufficient were – and still are – the regular teams. A band of experienced dressers will develop a distinctive approach to the use of materials and techniques that serves to identify their work almost as characteristically as the designer's flair: so much so that, when the latter changes, the style remains much the same. This is doubly beneficial: more obviously it means that the special appeal of the Youlgrave festival is not only that there are five different wells, there are five different experiences; less obviously it means that connoisseurs can make comparisons and preferences without offending the underlying, anti-competitive ethos.

---

[5] I still have a complete set of them on postcards sent to me by an aunt in 1945. I was 4,000 miles from home and I suppose she sought through her souvenirs for something to remind me of Youlgrave. I was not taking too much interest in welldressings at the time, but I mention it for the nostalgic value she – and perhaps all her generation – attached to it.

Coldwell – Margaret Fell (née Boardman).

Coldwell Tap is at the highest point of the village so, in the days when the water supply was gravity fed, nearby residents often had better reason than most to pray for water. The redundant tapspot, still there to be seen, no longer accommodates the welldressing screen, which is now relocated a few yards round the corner to avoid the traffic pinchpoint.

Margaret has designed this tap since 1950 and that may not be the most remarkable thing to say about her record. For a good deal of that time (25 years in fact), she has lived never less than a hundred miles away, first in Ormskirk, Lancashire, then in Cumbria. Starting with a skill that most designers would be happy to end with, she has never sat on her laurels nor has she been satisfied to rest secure in the achievement that, from her early days, set standards for the rest of the welldressing world and earned her the admiration of connoisseurs. She has looked for new techniques, new ways to advance the art of welldressing without compromising the basic discipline.

The Coldwell team, along with Bank Top and Holywell, observe what we like to think of as a Youlgrave tradition: it is strict adherence to biblical illustrations, both in text and picture, not found so conspicuously in any other village. It has to be said, the subject suits the Coldwell team. Margaret's artistry and the painstaking work of her colleagues are seen to good effect in the portrayal of dynamic scenes.

The team has two unusual features that in a more politically-sensitive context I might forbear to mention: they are all women and they work throughout the day. There is an interconnected explanation: the Trinity Girls Club executed the border for the 1949 Bank Top welldressing and then transferred to Coldwell. The Trinity Girls became – dare I mention it – housewives and in Youlgrave housewives tended not to be regulated by career constraints. There is good reason for offering this seemingly gratuitous observation: it may help the understanding of discerning visitors to know that the subject of their admiration is the work of delicate fingers.

28

Well, perhaps as may be. Whatever the historical explanation may once have been, the local domestic scene no longer sets the agenda, as Margaret herself explains: *"I have several 'guest' workers. Folks who were work-colleagues, one from Glasgow and one from Bolton, take a week's holiday and work fulltime. Three additionally come for two full days."*

She goes on to illustrate another characteristic that is far from unique in Youlgrave: *teamwork*. Every welldresser I know is a dedicated teamworker and I cannot remember ever hearing a word of dissent at a welldressing – discussion, yes, and only when invited. If people could work for pay as harmoniously as they work for love at a welldressing. the surgeries would be empty. Margaret again: *"My team are fantastic! once we used buttercups that were picked wet and had begun to look shabby by Friday evening. When we had literally finished someone said 'Those buttercups look tatty, shall we do them again?' I replied emphatically 'No, we are going home!' Next day, when the procession arrived at Coldwell, one of the team came up quietly and said 'Buttercups look well, don't they? We did them again last night after you went home.' Now that is what I call dedication!"*

For those who like to analyse technique, Margaret believes the 'hallmark' of her screens is *'realistic modelling of faces and limbs and a strong emphasis upon (hopefully) the skilful use of shading'*. Few will disagree.

Bank Top – Frederick W. Shimwell

The Bank Top screen is on its original tapspot site – or would be if the tapspot had not, itself, been moved across the road in the earlier part of the century. The mystery is not why the tapspot was moved so much as why it was put there in the first place. Hardly anybody lived on the north side and, even in the 1860s, the reason for having to cross the road at this blindspot with two buckets in hand can only have been to test Darwin's theory of the survival of the fittest.

Fred is the doyen of welldressing in Youlgrave, perhaps even the world. He took charge of Bank Top, almost by accident, 50 years ago and, in his case too, the length of his experience may not be the most remarkable feature of his achievement. Here is how he began: *"I have always dressed at Bank Top, even as a child[6] when we were only allowed to collect flowers, etc. I really started designing in 1949 when Margaret and I were asked to design Bank Top. It had not been dressed since 1939 because of the war, so we were really starting from scratch. We formed a combined team of Girls' Club and Bankside Ex-servicemen. Margaret and her girls did the border and I and the ex-service lads did the picture. We have carried on from there and now have a very settled team. it is noticeable that the ladies have come back after a few years when their children are growing up, so we all age together and encourage the younger end as we go."*

Fred, as ever, plays downstage and his account needs to be supplemented. He became a designer in 1949 only because he drew the short straw. Few can believe that such an outstanding talent could have had so inauspicious a beginning, yet records reveal that within a year or two he was changing the scope of welldressing art. Today his style, instantly recognisable, dramatic and colourful, may now be too familiar to raise eyebrows and it is only through the comparison of the photographic records that the measure of his innovations can be recognised.

All designers welcome visitors to the workshop, Fred especially. He believes there should always be someone free to explain to the uninitiated what is happening. The sites of welldressing workshops do change over the years so a location map might soon be out of date, but visitors who find the Bank Top workplace – currently at the Old Hall garage – can be sure of a cordial welcome. But they should beware! They won't be the first innocent sightseers to visit Fred and find themselves ensnared in a lifetime's addiction.

---

[6] Young Freddie is to be seen in the photograph of the 1927 Bank Top welldressing.

By the way ... this is a good place for anyone with energy to spare to experience the measure of benefit that piped water brought to the daily round. Walk through the jennel[7] alongside the old tapspot and begin the descent down into the dale (beware, it gets steeper!). On each side are the old cottages, many of them built out of limestone rubble by the leadminers in their spare time, sited more with an eye to aspect than prospect and with land economy very much in mind. The good news is that within three hundred metres or so, brave hearts will be rewarded with a lovely riparian scene – the bad news is that they will have crossed eight or nine 5-metre contours on the way down and will meet them again on the return trip. Perhaps it will be some encouragement to know that they won't have a full bucket of water in each hand. Now they have a good idea of what the arrival of the Bank Top tapspot meant to the people living on Bankside, even for those lower down, since it is a good deal easier to carry a full bucket down than up.

At the river's edge, where the bank is retained by a low wall, the declivity into which buckets were dipped and filled for domestic use can still be seen. A mile or so further upstream, effluent from Middleton ran into the watercourse so what else may have got into the Youlgrave buckets is anybody's guess and why pestilence didn't wipe out the population is a question for fastidious European regulators to ponder.

One reason why the custom of giving thanks for water prevails in this part of the world may be that our ancestors did not die drinking it. Carboniferous limestone, which is the bedrock of almost all the traditional welldressing villages, has a remarkable purifying effect on water[8] which is well illustrated by the history of Youlgrave's sewage disposal methods.

---

[7] the narrow passage between buildings known as a ginnel or jitty in less-enlightened places.

[8] Isaac Walton described the Lathkill as *the clearest stream in England.*

Although culverted sewerage did come to Youlgrave well before this century began, the refinement of a sewage works was left to later generations. Until thirty-odd years ago, the effluent was piped into disused mineshafts and, naturally, found its way into the mine de-watering system. Not a very edifying tale, it might be said, but I hope to show the point of it.

The mine de-watering system composed a network of soughs driven at great expense in the 18th century to reduce the cost of pumping water from the leadmines and thereby improve their economic viability. The most important of these was the Hill Carr Sough that reached the Alport Mining Company in 1787 and eventually drained the Youlgrave mines. It ran for 4½ miles under Stanton Moor and took 21 years to complete at a cost of £32,000 and the lives of several miners. For anyone interested enough to trace it, the outflow, still copious, emerges from an arched tail in the hillside close by Stanton Lees and – this is the point of the story – the burghers of Matlock, searching for a source of water for the town, came upon the outflow in the 1920s and had it analysed for potability. A Youlgrave district councillor who knew where the water began its journey, and was not about to call attention unnecessarily to such sanitary nonchalance, held his peace in the expectation that the chemists would save him the embarrassment. It was a vain hope; the water was found to be sparkling clear and biochemically blameless. Fortunately for his tranquil mind, the project was dropped for other reasons, but we welldressers can share with him a sense of gratitude for our limestone-purified springs and watercourses[9]. How much more grateful must our forbears have been when disease and pestilence caused other villages to be completely evacuated.

Here by the stream at the bottom of Holywell Lane is a good

---

[9] Blackley spring rises on the gritstone, of course, but there is, or was, no impurity of source to rectify.

place to linger for a while and sense the passage of time. The charming old clapper bridge gives a clue to the former importance of this ancient footway that winds up the hillside and bears the enigmatic name of *The Old Mouth*.[10] It was along this path that Eric Evans ran from his mother's cottage (now a cafe) in the afternoon of 23rd May, 1932, in a doomed attempt to rescue his workmates in the Shining Gutter Mine. Halfway into the climb a path rises off to the right and ascends to Mutlow Nab where, according to Mr. Stamper's dubious account, Oliver Cromwell set up his cannon and blasted Middleton Castle into ruin.

*   *   *   *   *   *

Holywell – John Marple

The first thing to say about Holywell, in all honesty, is that it is not what it sounds. Visitors will look in vain for a tapspot because the screen is now some forty yards away from the place where the tapdressing used to be. It is the most ornate of the tapspots and worth a close look, provided one eye is kept on the traffic hazard that caused it to be abandoned as a well-dressing location in the first place. It is easy to find by following the street wall of what is known as Barry's Croft[11].

Incidentally, the view from here encapsulates much of the relevant history of Youlgrave. Looking south across the valley to the gritstone outcrop is the spoil heap of the old Shining Gutter leadmine. To its left is the woodland source of the village springwater. About twenty degrees further left, in view over the roof of the village hall, is a flattened eminence on the

---

[10] A few hundred yards upstream is the hillside entrance to an old drift mine with the equally-intriguing name of *Nelly Longarm's Cave*.

[11] After the one time owner of the Old Hall opposite. This distinguished house on Main Street, formerly known as Hopton House, is said to be the scene of a Civil War fracas with a fatal outcome, which is claimed to recur as a phantom action-replay.

skyline. This is the site of an iron Age fort, behind which lies Harthill Moor. It is a symbolic prospect.

The immediate postwar relocation of the screen to its present position in front of the Wesleyan Reform Chapel actually enhanced its *well*dressing – as opposed to its *tap*dressing – credentials: a few yards from the chapel gate is the site of one of the old wells. It was approached by steps and, being below ground level, can no longer be seen. The temptation to link the welldressing with the place of worship has to be resisted: they have no historical association and, in any case, the name Holywell belongs to the lane that is more historically called Holloway Lane. Perhaps I should have allowed visitors to keep their illusion.

John Marple is a relative newcomer to the welldressing scene and the only non-homegrown designer. He came to live in Youlgrave in 1993 and joined the Holywell team as a novice. On Jim's untimely death in 1997 he was the popular choice to succeed him. He demurred, of course, on the grounds of being a *new boy* but (and this is a significant demonstration of the division of responsibility in a settled group) it was pointed out that the team had experience to spare; his qualifications as an architect and artist were a more compelling argument. Now, two welldressings later and his diffidence banished by success, he takes his place in Youlgrave's hall of fame.

Visitors will hardly notice the change of designer, which is not surprising since the appearance – as opposed to the design – owes most to the style of the team. A feature of the *Holywell* screen is brilliant colour contrasts and sharp divisions, which was very much Jim's recognisable signature. Like Margaret and Fred, he belonged to what might be impertinently called the *Bible School* and was even more of a traditionalist in regard to style. While they depict movement in their scenes, Jim conveyed the static quality of a biblical scene in a Sunday school book, a long-ago timelessness that was a feature of bygone welldressings. Having learned to dress wells under Jim's guidance, John is unlikely to depart from the customary *Holywell* presentation.

The Fountain – Nicholas Stacey

The first thing that has to be said about *The Fountain* is that it is different. One reason for the difference, which I daresay they will forgive me for mentioning, is that it has no familiar signature. Whereas the other four taps have seen only one change of designer in a generation, the Fountain has seen ten in the last 20 years. The more obvious consequence is that the unexpected can be expected.

A regular visitor once told me that when he approached the *Fountain* screen, he did so with his eyes half-closed and averted so as not to dissipate the sense of surprise and pleasure he knew he would experience at close range. I knew what he meant. While we can be sure the other four taps will be magnificent, each in its own way, we can forecast exactly how they will be so. Not so with the *Fountain*. I have seen arcadian screens, gothic screens, mediaeval screens, renaissance screens, post-impressionist screens. I recall screens from the early 1970's that were stunning in their brilliance and originality; I recall other screens where the unorthodox approach misfired. There was even a time, decades ago, when it more than once caused a furore. Come what may, *The Fountain* has never been dull and – this perhaps better whispered – those who seek arcane manifestations will surely find them closest to the surface of a *Fountain* screen.

Why, it may be asked? should this flair for innovation and experiment be so much a feature of *The Fountain*? Almost certainly it has its roots in the succession of passing designers, none of whom had lived long in the village or possessed a welldressing background. Artistry and execution in these circumstances tend to be separate functions, separate skills, the artist (designer) being unconfined by ritual constraints, yet having a team equal to the challenge of interpretation. In 1979, the distinguished artist, John Piper, with no previous knowledge of welldressing, consented to design the *Fountain* screen for the 150th anniversary of the Youlgrave Waterworks. Opinions may differ on the outcome, so I offer it more as an

35

interesting fact than as proof of the theory.

Nick presided over his second design this year. He is is a native-born virtuoso whose formal art education ended with A-level. Although still in his mid-twenties, he can claim 19 years welldressing experience, so he must be considered a good bet one day to emulate Fred and Margaret.

The Church – Ruth McGrath (née Mercer)
The old tap-spot site, not all that long out of service, associated with this screen is still easily traced in the west wall of the Reading Room across the road. The reason for the comparatively recent re-location probably had less to do with traffic than with shade. Whatever the reason, nestling as it does against the north face of the church tower, it seems so convenient and appropriate a place to be that one can only wonder at the power of tradition that kept it so firmly anchored where it was for more than a hundred years. *The Reading Room Tap* is what it was – and still is in the minds of older residents – until 1977. It is the most significant of the four welldressing taps and ranks only marginally below *The Fountain* in historical importance.

Ruth is the third generation of her family to design this screen. Her maternal grandfather, Samuel Nuttall, was in charge from the turn of the century to the Great War; her father, Nick Mercer, held the fort between 1957 and 1972, after which Ruth took over. With her own children taking a keen interest, she is hoping to extend what must already be a three-generation record into a fourth. Ruth, living in Shifnal, Shropshire for the last 17 years and with a family to raise, has mastered the art of welldressing by remote control. Perhaps it is not by coincidence that she shares one other experience with Margaret:

> *"Our team is very small and we only have one member who is truly 'local'. One stalwart dresser who has left the area returns each year from York on a daily basis to contribute along with*

her mother from Wales. Neither is a Youlgrave 'native'. I believe this commitment to the tradition is, in itself; quite remarkable."

Surprisingly, despite the huge commitment of Ruth and her family to this tap, it is to two other designers that we must turn for their conspicuous influence on the wider front. Edwin Shimwell changed its face, an influence we shall be examining in closer detail; Harold Lees kept the Youlgrave custom alive through the distractions of war, but for which it might have died. And as the village headmaster, following the precedent set by his predecessor (G.W. Gimber), he and his wife Doris provided a vital link between welldressing and the children.

Mr. Lees, as he was universally known amongst pupils and adults alike, was one of the old school of traditionalists, choosing biblical scenes and texts as his subjects. Photographs of them have an old-fashioned look, even in 1956, by which time Fred and Margaret had been breaking new ground further west for seven years. In the two years following his retirement his successor, Nick Mercer, made only subtle alterations, but 1959 saw a conspicuous change to a style that has since become a landmark for visitors. Out went the biblical portrayal; in came the contemporary picture book look. In, too, came one other enduring innovation: *1959* became *MCMLX* and, whatever the reason for the change, the *Reading Room Church* remains the only screen in the village with a Roman datemark. Ruth officially took charge in 1973, after two years in double harness with her father, with no noticeable change in style.

Most visitors will recognise the style as markedly different from the other screens. What they may not discern is how fundamental is the difference: it is not just a case of looking different, it is *theologically* different. The three westernmost taps are severely Judaeo-Christian. They have no message of their own to convey, merely a reminder of what the bible has to say, warts and all. *The Church tap* has its own message, sentimentally expressed, that argues intrinsic goodness through a world of

37

innocent children. It is a repudiation of the doctrine of Original Sin – and visitors are very comfortable with it.

Although the same motif has recurred regularly since 1965, Ruth denies any significance: *"Whilst I do think the Reading Room Well is distinguishable from the others, and indeed each well is very individual, I cannot attribute this to any particular aspect. Although the well predominantly features a child or children, this is not a deliberate aim. Rather, the attempt is to have an overall theme incorporating both picture and borders. Designs were always a subject for family discussion, which developed into a partnership before I took over. I have just carried on from there."*

As well as creating considerable appeal and affection among visitors, it generates a popular misconception. Inclined to refer to it as *The Children's Well*, they confuse subject matter with handiwork. It is, of course, a misnomer. The idea of a well-dressing of this quality and competence being designed and executed by young welldressers is a compliment difficult to resist, but resisted it must be. The notion of a team based on youth and inexperience would violate a basic precept of well-dressing practice in Youlgrave.

* * * * * *

Requiem ... Most people begin, rather than end, their half-mile-long welldressing excursion here, which is a pity: like most country churchyards it is a good place to rest awhile in contemplation. A few yards out ot sight is the serene and peaceful ambience of the south porch, and what better place to end a welldressing experience than where *the rude forefathers of the hamlet sleep.*

Not a few of them were bedded down by Sam B., the sexton some eighty years ago, who by the evidence of this authentic, first-hand account, was clearly not overawed by the gravity of his calling.

It was polling day in a parliamentary election, many years ago. The polling station was in the school, adjoining the churchyard, and one or two cars had been busy during the morning bringing in the halt and the lame, the decrepit and feeble who, by all appearances, would soon exhaust their last reserves of strength in the act of putting a cross on the voting slip. This activity, if it can be so called, did not escape the notice of Sam, who was watching for a while from the church-yard steps with his shovel over his shoulder, when the candidate arrived to *show the rosette*. He walked over to Sam and said *"I hope you're going to vote."* *"Well"* Sam replied, pointing his shovel toward a tottering voter, *"Ah likely will, but ah were just wonderin' ... mun ah[12] go an' dig thee toothrie[13] up?"* The candidate, let it be said, took it in good humour and as they parted. Sam struck a fine balance between deference and political partiality. *"Ah wish thee the best o' luck, me Lord,"* he said. *"an' ah 'ope thah loses."* Sam, you see, was a Whig.

---

[12] Must I

[13] Toothrie is vaguely dismissive expression no longer much in use. It stems from *two* or *three,* but these numerical values have no significance, the quantity varies with tone and content. Nobody **knows** how many it means, **everybody** understands it.

Coldwell

Selecting any one year from the records to illustrate the achievement of the Coldwell team is tantamount to picking a single piece of jewellery from Aladdin's cave. Their work has been a constant joy to visitors and a source of pride to the local residents, even those who have never placed a petal nor thought to do so. Rated purely on visual impact, almost any year would serve as well as the next, but this 1982 screen is a paragon for anyone whose interest extends to the composition and forethought that inspired it. It typifies the research and draughtsmanship that is but one outstanding feature of the Coldwell contribution.

The average reader will be better qualified to analyse its artistic qualities. The accuracy of shape and perspective are obviously the hallmark of the designer; the precise execution of detail and shading, for which Coldwell is renowned, owes as much to the patient, nimble fingers of the ladies who comprise her team – and, of course, the time dedicated to applying them.

Coldwell screens inevitably tinge the admiration of visitors with a sense of poignancy. Here is a picture that would grace the Royal Academy destined to live for less than a week. But it is this ephemeral nature of welldressings that raises them from pleasing spectacle to fleeting transcendence.

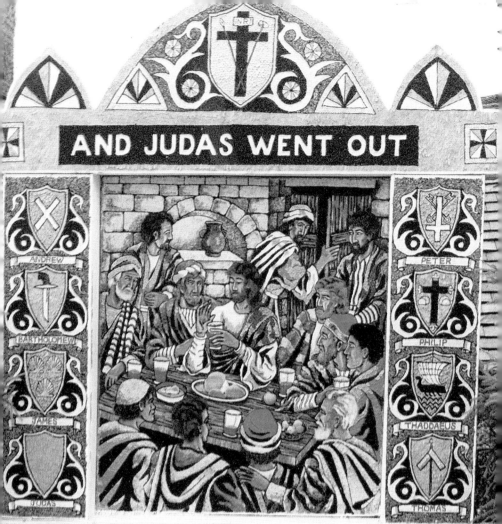

AND JUDAS WENT OUT

Bank Top

Set a Bank Top screen in any other location and the flair would be instantly recognisable (See Chapter 6 Brunnenschmuckeren*). Dramatic movement in welldressing is seldom attempted and even less frequently achieved, yet the work of the Bank Top team is instantly-recognisable by a style that must be the envy of designers everywhere who aspire to dynamic effect. The borders, in contrast, tend to be serene and soothing, although the colours are always integrated with the picture and can sometimes be riveting in themselves. The floral designs of other years are particularly distinctive, but Fred denies any attempt to improve on nature. The striking artistic effect may deflect attention from the meticulous handiwork that produces a Bank Top screen. There are no shortcuts. Flesh-portrayal apart, every inch of the screen is covered in a traditional material and petals are used wherever practicable – evidence the painstaking blend of dried hydrangea petals used to create the horses when a less-exacting choice could have been excused. Such meticulous coverage undoubtedly contributes to the lasting quality of the clay, although the durability of the screen owes something to the shaded location. Incidentally, the tapspot – easily detected behind the screen – was across the road in earlier photographs, so this is one of the two tap dressings that has not been, of necessity, separated from its functional setting.*

43

Holywell

This is not a typical Holywell screen, described previously as renowned for "brilliant colour contrasts", more marked in years when there is a profusion of the favoured blooms – hydrangeas, geraniums and buttercups – but it does portray another distinctive feature: unlike the other two adherents to the Biblical School, Holywell has a static image – the timelessness of a posed photograph that captures a single moment in time. It is more representative of a tapestry than a painting. It is probably the most conventional of the Youlgrave screens, although the modern style of integrating picture and border is a feature.

As a rule, almost every device in Jim's borders had a symbolic or religious significance, not always Judaeo-Christian despite his personal commitment, and he would sometimes include a discreet reference to a secular event that he considered worth a special mention. In this case loyalty got the better of him on both counts.

44

THE QUEENS SILVER JUBILEE

1977

THE ANOINTING OF DAVID

The Fountain

There is no such thing as a typical Fountain screen, unless the unexpected can be described as typical, so the task of finding a representative example is correspondingly difficult. Should it feature the innovative use of materials – most evident in this case by the use of opened-up straw in the cap – or should it emphasise the imaginative juxtasposition of colours and textures? These are the stock-in-trade of the Fountain team to be found in almost any illustration. It is the influence of successive designers whose unrestrained and often brilliant portrayals make the selection so open-ended.

*This brilliantly unorthodox screen, designed by Jim Connolly in 1973, may not be everyone''s first choice from the album of this Tap – perhaps not even that of the Fountain practitioners themselves – but it is chosen as much for the year as for the subject. A whole generation separates us from this ground-breaking experiment, innovative even by today's standards, yet it conformed with the conventions of the time. **For the record, the immediate past generation of Fountain designers – in chronological succession – are Jim Connolly, D. Weston/C. Prince, Malcolm Nix, John Piper, Rosalind Forster, Alastair Scrivener, Karen Sayer and Irris Pimm.***

19 THE ANNUNCIATION 73

MCMLXXXII

I will lift up mine eyes
unto the hills...

The Church

This example of The Church dressing is chosen for no other reason than its photogenic quality. Almost any example from the records would suffice to illustrate the particular style and content, which sets out to be appealing, rather than impressive, and adheres to an idyllic, picture-book format. It is known by visitors as The Children's Well because it usually features juveniles, but the work is clearly that of a talented, adult team, albeit a small one.

Both in subject matter and execution it is quite distinct from the other four taps. The materials are used differently and applied in cameo form. Look for the artistic effect of a comprehensive theme incorporating both picture and borders. The technique is by no means unusual in Youlgrave, nor even original, but it does tend to be more spectacular here because an unconventional theme lends itself to a range of motifs in the border that are especially striking. They never illustrate a biblical scene and rarely carry a biblical text (this being an exception): freedom from these constraints provides the canvas for the pretty and appealing presentations.

Ruth affirms that her designs are not subject-oriented but, viewed in gallery, the records reveal a consistent pattern. They invariably depict natural goodness seen through the innocence of children. Judging by the unfailing popularity of the tap, it finds a receptive audience.

Chapter 3
WELLDRESSERS AT WORK

Youlgrave welldressers harbour a secret fear – well, not a fear really, more amused speculation – that the midsummer sun will one Saturday morning dawn on five identical welldressings. The possibility is less a reflection on the law of averages than a comment on the compartmented structure of the organisation. Yes, the Committee[1] – there is always a committee – is there to take care of the routine arrangements, but in all other respects the autonomy of each *tap* is absolute and jealously guarded. Each has its separate sphere of operation and each functions spontaneously.

A favourite cliché of writers is *the mystery of welldressing.* As far as Youlgrave is concerned, a small component of the mystery must seem to be how the *taps* come to be dressed each year – in time – on time. There is no deliberate mustering; the designer turns up to the venue fully-equipped with accessories and the team assemble like swallows answering the call of the wild. People who may not have seen each other to speak to for

---

[1] It used to comprise representatives appointed from each tap (three each from The Reading Room and Fountain, two each from the rest). Nowadays any bone fide welldresser who cares to turn up to a meeting is a committee member. It sounds like a recipe for anarchy, but Peter Pimm, Jim's secretarial successor, masters it with aplomb.

11 months appear at their habitual venue and greet each other with *"What are we on this year, then?"* Some may have come from far afield, perhaps having spent the winter giving illustrated talks to audiences who have never seen a welldressing; others may have given it scarcely a thought. There are those who were born in the village, those who have come to live in the village and those who probably never will. Nature calls and they answer.

It is a playful exaggeration, of course: the countdown to Midsummer began several weeks before the post-hibernation stirrings and a village the size of Youlgrave has a grapevine that misses nothing. The first overt stirring is the taking of the boards to soak in the river.[2] Simon turns up with his tractor and trailer and, if lucky, with a team of sturdy helpers, retrieves the boards from their store in the Pinfold and carts them off down Holywell Lane to the River Bradford where they are unloaded and left to soak midstream. A board is a large wooden tray that holds a $\frac{1}{2}$ to $\frac{3}{4}$" layer of clay; there is the main picture board, usually two side-boards (longer and narrower), a head board and a base board – five boards to a tap – which it can be imagined displaces a fair volume of river water and creates disquiet among the passing endurance walkers on the Limestone Way.[3] *"Just look at that,"* one was once heard to say, *"dumping their rubbish in this beautiful stream. They're not fit to live here."* It is only a temporary desecration if only they did but know it. Ten days later, the boards are gone, but not until the passers-by are confronted with yet another example of local sacrilege. Several families are gathered for a picnic on the riverbank and, having set up their tables, are now being merrily diverted in a mud-throwing contest which,

[2] To prevent dry boards soaking moisture from the clay.

[3] The Limestone Way was conceived in the 1980's by an organisation looking for something to do. Its success cannot be denied, always supposing the original intention had been to develop the human herd instinct.

since the contestants have come prepared with protective (now-bespattered) clothing, is clearly no accident of sudden abandon. Even more cranky, it turns out, they are throwing the mud not at each other – at least, not intentionally – but at the picnic tables. If only the watchers will linger awhile, they will see the floats and trowels come out to begin the serious business of smoothing the clay – for *clay* it is, of course – onto the wooden boards. The welldressers are *claying* up.

The multi-village welldressing fraternity are well-disposed and open to each other as a rule; the winning of clay is a conspicuous exception. It is, these days, such a scarce commodity that if a village finds a useful source it becomes tight-lipped about it. After years of ready bounty from the local brickworks and, lately, a more distant pottery, Youlgrave finds itself having to be conservation-minded. The clay – or such proportion as can be salvaged – is recycled from one year to the next. It is a tiresome process that, to susceptible minds, has ritual connotations: the life-cycle of a welldressing, created with patience and care from Monday to Friday, should fittingly end in the counterpoise of careless destruction the following Friday. It somehow seems unworthy to be picking over the pieces.

* * * * * *

Balaams ass ... Before we follow Simon and his loaded trailer up into the village. we may recall it was here, once more, by the old clapper bridge that Jimmy T. cursed the 9th Duke of Rutland.

Jimmy was a local *character*. Grown restless in his family's successful business, he spotted (in today's parlance) what he perceived to be a niche in the market and set up as a travelling greengrocer, hawking fruit and vegetables around the villages from a donkey cart. Jimmy was irrepressible and, like all village *characters*, his exploits enlivened the daily round. One such involved the donkey he kept to draw his fruit and vegetable cart. I know not whether the donkey had a name but it reportedly had a temperament as stubborn as its master's was volatile And it clearly had no great enthusiasm for greengrocery. It grazed offduty on the hillside south of the River Bradford and, well aware of what awaited it on the other side, firmly resisted Jimmy's attempts to get it across the clapper bridge of a morning. Jimmy was not a patient man; it took only a brief spell of asinine intransigence before he would set to and *curse* the donkey and, since *Jimmy cursing the donkey* made a lively start to the day, housewives on Bankside would come out for the entertainment. One morning, the scene was enhanced by the arrival of the Duke on his way upstream for a spot of fishing. The Duke, his sense of propriety getting the better of his discretion, intervened on behalf of the ladies in the audience, who were immediately rewarded with the added spectacle of *Jimmy cursing the Duke.* As for His Grace, he apparently went on his way suitably chastened and there was the end of the matter, at least so far as he was concerned. Jimmy then took to parking the donkey on the village side of the river. This hillside, as will be seen, is even more precipitous and certainly a good deal less convenient for Jimmy. He had to tether the donkey halfway down and scramble to the stream to fetch it a bucket of water, which of course the donkey scorned to drink. Jimmy tried coaxing, he tried cursing and, finally, when all approaches had been rebuffed, he flung the water in the donkey's face crying *"Thah musn't think because thah'rt a donkey that Jimmy's one as well."*

The tale has a sad sequel. One morning, the donkey was found strangled by its tether. It had wandered too far and, undonkeylike, slipped over a small rock. It was an accident, of that there can be no doubt, yet ... the thought of a life of altercation with Jimmy must have been hard to bear, even for a donkey.

* * * * * *

But here on the riverbank this Monday evening, the boards are *clayed-up* and ready to be delivered to their respective workshops. There is no time to reminisce. Time is vital in the creation of a welldressing screen and the work must proceed according to an almost inflexible timetable. An expert's summary is provided in Appendix 1, but here is a timetable for the benefit of the visitor who, having seen the completed screens, is of a mind to see one made:

Monday evening – the screen usually comprises a picture board, two side boards, a head board and base (all standing about eight feet high when erected) which are taken indoors and laid flat on trestles. Margaret initially stands her picture board upright, the better to create true perspectives in outline, then lays it flat. Some villages use this *in situ* method throughout. There are good arguments for it, just as there are equally good reasons for having the screens indoors, well-lit and sheltered from wind and rain. At this stage, there is only the *marking out* to be done. The smooth clay surface is overlaid with paper templates through which the designs are pricked[4] into the clay.

Tuesday: Liners, traditionally blacknobs (alder cones), beans and maize (though the trend in Youlgrave has been to break with tradition and use black knitting wool) are then pressed into the pattern of perforations to highlight the design. Picture animation begins with the insertion of non-perishable materials such as lichen.

Wednesday: More of the same, including semi-perishables like parsley.

Thursday: Less tender leaves and petals are incorporated.

Friday: The most tender materials are worked into the design.

---

[4] Coldwell have a different technique, claimed to have been introduced by The Fountain. They linemark the design outline on the underside of the template and transfer it straight onto the clay.

So in the course of a week, a section of a picture – say a robe – will develop like this.

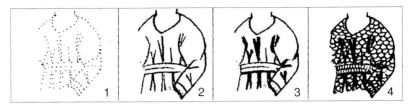

1 *The outline of folds has been pricked through from templates.*
2 *Traces have been lined with black knitting wool.*
3 *Shading has been created with reversed moss.*
4 *Hydrangea petals have been tiled into the clay.*

The build-up has two basic techniques, one practical the other artistic. Good practice requires petals to be overlapped like slates on a roof, in case of rain, and to cover the maximum surface of clay for the opposite reason – to prevent it drying out. The direction of petalling is a trap for the unwary: hours of painstaking work has had to be unpicked because daydreaming welldressers forgot they were working *upside-down* on the picture. The second maxim is always to remember that this is a painting of sorts. Nothing should be allowed to represent itself or to stand out from the surface in three-dimensional form, arguably because the *real* bit invalidates the rest of the portrayal. It is a subtle convention, not universally observed, so critics may find examples for themselves.

I have never seen a bar chart for a welldressing programme and I doubt any designer has ever been so methodical as to produce one. Faith and hope prevail over timetables; occasional spells of designer anxiety are well concealed. The Coldwell team seems to come closest to controlling the course of events, as Margaret explains: "*We work on the basis of using just those materials which 'last' best and bringing everything on together, border and picture concurrently. We aim to get on with it, the target always being to finish by 9 p.m. on Friday night, and we usually get close to that. It is my opinion that nobody does her best work when under pressure; if the finishing off goes late into the night, there is a danger of "anything goes" when desperation takes over. For the same reason I like to get the background in early – it's just as important as the subject matter and I prefer to get the more boring bits done while folks have the time and enthusiasm to take pains with it."*

What Margaret means by "anything goes' *when desperation takes over"'* is that there are certain expedients that welldressers may resort to when still faced with areas of naked clay late on Friday night. The *point at which desperation took over* is not difficult to detect in a finished screen. Sorrel seed and lime dust are usually – not always – evidence of expediency, although it is a long time since I saw the latter in a Youlgrave screen. But here a plea for tolerance: villages that dress early in the season may have their options directed less by scarcity of time than materials.

Material concern ... The use of materials has long been a focus for controversy. What is and what is not *allowable* is, to some welldressers, a matter of kosher-like prescription. *Only natural materials* says one. Another will find this too permissive: it has to be materials that *"grow naturally"*. And so it goes – on the one hand contentious, on the other necessary, because without a basic discipline it ceases to command respect as a unique artform. The trick is not to let the rules get in the way of artistic expression.

There has been criticism from other villages that Youlgrave designers have taken liberties in the use of materials and I think that is a perfectly valid point of view for anyone who expects welldressing to remain frozen in time – although at which point down the ages the development should be frozen is never explained. What is undeniable is that the innovation and experiment of which the Youlgrave designers have been leading exponents have raised the calibre of welldressing art throughout the district – in fact the world.

Take, for example. the technique for outlining the shapes:

"Some folk may look on the use of wool for outlining as not tradition-al," says Margaret. *"I favour it because I believe outlining to be about the most critical stage (you can never improve on what you achieve at this stage). Wool allows a clear, even line and smooth-flowing curves which individual beans or blacknobs never could".*

Despite a sentimental attachment to blacknobs, I have to concede the logic. Of course, there have to be rules. My own belief. for what it is worth, is that nothing should be used that would not or could not have been used by our forbears and its appearance should remain unaltered once it has been applied.

With one exception the Youlgrave teams tend to be conserv-ative in their use of materials. Hydrangeas, Buttercups and Dog Daisies are the staple blooms; moss, parsley and ever-greens fill the spaces. *The Fountain* is the exception and they differ as much in the way they use the standard materials as in their introduction of the new.

All villages seem to have their own orders of preference and, having regard to the length of the welldressing season (May to September), it is easy to see how choice became gov-erned by availability. It is a limitation for which allowances are not always made as generously as they might be. In a bad year the dearth of flowers in May is a bane for the early well-dressers who, in making do with what they have, are given less credit for achievement than their less florally-challenged neighbours. Youlgrave has either the good fortune, or the good sense – to benefit from a more plentiful season. Or does it? During the last few years, there has been a perceptible change in natural flowering patterns that disturbs even our ancient routine: the once plentiful Buttercup has now passed its peak by midsummer and even Hydrangeas may be in short supply.

Although the choice of materials has remained much the same in Youlgrave for as long as most people can remember, the way in which they are used is a feature of the modern kind of presentation. Whereas, say fifty years ago, they were used to *adorn* the picture, now they are used to *create* it. The old designers seemed to give more thought to where they were putting the blacknobs than to what they intended to put inside them.

Magaret again: *"I believe in buying the minimum of flowers and of using what is available to best advantage. To this end I try to have a very flexible approach to the colour scheme and deliberately resist the temptation to plan for colours that may prove difficult to obtain (e.g. scarlet or strong blue). I accept, for instance, that it is appropriate to buy a blue Hydrangea (if you can get one) to do a sky, but in my view pastel pinks and blues are in no way essential to a border and inappropriate to Biblical gowns – surely in Biblical times strong earthy colours would be the order of the day. We are keen to introduce as much colour as possible before even coming to petals. For one reason, leaves being usually more robust have better keeping properties, but equally have just as much to contribute colour-wise. Take variegated Box, for example: the dark old growth, the new fresh green of the current year's growth and the clear yellow top growth produce a feast of colour. The same goes for Berberis – dark maroon old leaves, rich deep new growth and positively scarlet tips. plus the tones of pale fawn to orange in the middle of the bush where they have been denied the light – surely rivalling Wallflowers in their range of richness and tone. Texture, too, is important to the choice of materials; Rhubarb seed to represent a sheepskin cloak, for example – just the right off-white shade and curly look to it."*

Needless to say. the idea of using sheepskin itself is something she and the other designers would find incomprehensible.

Protection ... The function of petals and the like is by no means entirely decorative. We tend to regard them in the same way as fashionable clothes and, in admiring their decorative quality, we overlook their more practical function which, for the most part, is to cover up. In the case of welldressing materials, it is the clay that has to be covered, not just because bare clay has little artistic merit in the raw state but because, uncovered, it dries out and cracks more readily. Hydrangeas are very popular as much for their physical characteristics as for their colour; like dog daisies, they will not shrink and curl up to expose the clay beneath.

Sometimes there is no alternative but to leave a bare clay finish where the flesh of arms, legs and faces are portrayed. The portrayal of hair is a useful though limited device: critics will allow that male biblical faces were mostly bearded but will draw the line at concealing the faces of women and children by the same device. As for arms, there is a limit to the number of times that Esau can be summoned into service. Hence the subterfuge of welldressers everywhere, including the strict fundamentalists, who proscribe all but that which *grows*. How did this face get its colour and whence those muscles and features?

One last word on the subject of materials and clay, the worst thing that can be said about Youlgrave welldressings is that their shelf-life is abysmal. There is always at least one starting to crack by Tuesday and the frailty is a matter of current anxiety.

Equal opportunities, and that ... The visitor who decides to see for himself will be more than welcome at any of the workplaces. but first he has to find one. Unlike the tapspots where the screens will be prominently displayed, the erstwhile workshops are tucked away in sheds and garages with the only outward and visible sign of anything unusual taking place being an inevitable knot of children hovering around the entrance. These are the budding welldressers, too young yet to have welldressing *stickability* but ready and willing to take off on a flower-gathering mission. They are not to be discouraged: this is how four of Youlgrave's five designers began their distinguished careers.

Inside, a group of anything between ten and thirty people is spread around apparently at random but, in reality. very much focused on the several components of the screen. The numbers vary not only from tap to tap but also according to the time of day and the day of the week. The teams are fluid: people come and go, picking up where they left off or, just as readily, taking over some incompleted section from someone else.

The disposal is not so random as it looks. Take *Holywell*, for instance: that pair working side by side and apparently self-absorbed are not together by accident; the older one is keeping a very discreet eye on the beginner. On-the-job instruction has its own protocol in welldressing: every novice will be a potential designer only so long as confidence and natural skill are allowed to develop. Jim, an ex-teacher, had the patience of his profession. Anyone with a serious interest child or adult, was found a job in the Arrowdale Farm garage at dressing time, guided patiently but never discouraged by overt supervision and always left rewarded by the pride of being able to point out to friends and family some corner of a finished screen and say: *"I did that!"* The chances are he/she didn't. Late on Friday evening, long after all but the most dedicated workers have retired, Jim has often unpicked some small area and re-redressed it to standard, for-bearing to mention or correct it in the presence of the well-inten-tioned perpetrator. Nobody need know.

The casual visitor, particularly to *Holywell*, may fail to notice intriguing evidence of sexual segregation. Though less rigidly observed than ten years ago, there is a convention that women work on the border and men work on the picture. It is the ves-tige of a very interesting, practice that, fortunately, lost curren-cy in time to avoid the rebuke of today's *PC* punctilio. Until the end of the 1930's, welldressing was the exclusive domain of the menfolk. The ladies were involved only in fashioning the garlands round the picture. The exclusion seems to be related to a presumption that work (as in paid employment) was specifically the duty of men. Strange as it may seem, well-dressing appears to have ranked as paid work. A clue to this was provided by Mrs. Marion Alport, daughter of Edwin Shimwell of whom we shall learn more later. She said, to my surprise, that her father, a man with austere views on well-dressing, was in favour of men being paid because *"they some-times had to take time off work to do it."* It casts new light on some old arguments and there are interesting wider implications.

yet to be examined.

Margaret's postwar experience reveals an improvement in the lot of lady welldressers – of necessity, I suspect – and it was a case of *effect* surviving *cause*. *"In those early days we were **paid** for welldressing! At other Taps it was a fixed sum – so much per man, **less** for a woman and* something for each child. *The sums involved were quite small and bore no relation to the work involved.*[5] *At Coldwell (the last dressing to be reinstated after the war) there was an elaborate points system by which the team were all paid according to the amount of work they put in. As a designer I got top pay, which I think amounted to something like £1.10.0 (old money).*[6]

Although the Youlgrave ladies had to await their welldressing suffrage a good deal longer than Mrs. Pankhurst, they did eventually prevail... well, they are getting there. Garland to border was an easy progression; between border and picture board lay – and still lie – more persistent inhibitions. One evening not all that long ago, a young lady new to the village and in blissful ignorance of welldressing decorum, joined the men on the picture board. Now. the volume of chatter at a fullscale welldressing session is only obvious when it stops. It stopped. The men on the picture board were pleasantly surprised – nay, flattered to be joined, but it was not allowed to last: one of the other ladies gathered the would-be intruder and led her quietly away to her proper station in life. l am not making it up, it really happened. Things are different now but old habits die hard.

The ticking clock ... By Thursday at *Holywell*, the question is

---

[5] Paltry though this sum may have been, it was nevertheless the cause of a far-from-paltry *to-do* in the 1950's.

6 In earlier times, dressers at some *taps* were known to take their reward in advance. A firkin of ale set up handily before the work began avoided an excess of *downtime* spent travelling to and from the pub on the Friday night – at least, that would have been the *time and motion study* excuse. It may also provide a less irritating explanation for the exclusion of women to those who fret about discrimination.

voiced with increasing frequency by casual visitors: *How is it going? Are you up to time?* The ladies will state quite positively that they are – they always are – and the men on the picture will hedge. It is not a reflection on sexual disparity in either competence or outlook. Progress on the border is quantifiable because, once the materials are selected, the work is largely mechanical and evenly spaced. Progress on the picture. however cannot be measured by the area of clay covered. There are easy parts and hard parts; parts that can be covered quickly early in the week and parts that must be held back; it is *make-it-up-as-you-go-progress*, with a fair bit of standing, back and head scratching to punctuate it.

Friday night is welldressing to the death. It must be completed by dawn, even if it takes all night to do it. With luck the men will manage a few hours sleep before they fall in again at 6 a.m. in order to carry the boards to their showplace and erect them for all to see. *Men again*, it will be noted, but this time the discrimination should be acceptable to even the most militant monitor: muscle power is the overt explanation but I suspect that the ladies have no wish to be within earshot if the unthinkable should happen and a board were to crash out of hand to the ground. The fact that it never has, so far as l know, in no way lessens the chances that it might. Nowadays there will probably be a tractor and trailer – perhaps even a hydraulic hoist available to make life easier, a far cry from the days, not so long gone, when the *Holywell* boards were conveyed on an undertaker's handcart.

*   *   *   *   *   *

Undertaker's handcart! Well, a joiner's handcart really. When Jim told it to me in the lowered tones of a penitent in the confessional who cannot quite keep the smile off his face, I leapt to the bizarre conclusion that the handcart had occasionally served as a conveyance for the lately late on their way from the deathbed to the funeral parlour, wherever that might have been. It was an ordinary-looking two-wheeled flatbed – not the smart bier used for funerals – and the unwitting onlooker would see nothing odd in its use as a welldressing conveyor. Of course, I had jumped to the wrong conclusion; the only funeral parlour in those days was a flight of stairs below the deathbed and the handcart served only to convey the unoccupied – and therefore less riveting – coffin to the penultimate resting place.

Nevertheless, it serves as an illustration, not thought taste-less I hope, of how much more there was in the street-scene in those days. It used to belong to people – not vehicles – and everyone seemed to be carrying something or other, a bucket more often than not. It might contain water from the tapspot, foodstuffs for animals and chickens (*going to feed the hens*) or, if the pails hung on a yoke, the contents would be milk.[7] If it wasn't a bucket, it might be a *stick.* Men were forever carrying *sticks*, which was the generic term for any piece, or pieces, of wood from bundles of brushwood peasticks to the bole of a fallen tree. l suppose they (the sticks, that is) are now just left to rot in the woods.

There were some heroic *stickers.* Billy B. must have been the 1930's version of a redundant miner, happy to turn his hand to whatever would bring in a copper in cash or kind and forever foraging for home. He was a compact, roundish sort of man who invariably wore the bowler hat of the leadminer and could be frequently seen trudging along under a log the size of the bottom half of a ship's mast, dwarfed by his burden like some leaf-bearing ant. At other times, he would be seen about his business as a chimney sweep, carrying on his bicycle a bundle of rods long enough to sweep the church chimney, had he been called on unexpectedly to do so. He was hardly ever

---

[7] Until milk-marketing regulations put a stop to it, there must have been ten part-time farmers living in the village (a reminder of the days when lead-miners victualled their families with an agricultural sideline) who milked a cow or two in the stone sheds you now see crumbling in the fields. They brought the milk home to cool and sell to neighbours by the jugful.

Anyone over forty familiar with Youlgrave welldressing habits will find sufficient clues in this oldish photograph to place it almost precisely in time and place. Do-it-yourself detectives should read no further.

Clue 1. *The picture that Jim and stalwarts of* **Holywell***, brothers Colin and Ronald Brassington, are working on has been fully-lined and the filling begun with the most durable materials – reversed moss to provide the shading; it is too advanced to be the first night, so it must be* **Tuesday***.*

Clue 2. *Three at work on the picture is less than half a normal complement, so the men have not yet come home from work and had their tea (Jim is probably taking a week's holiday, Colin is self-employed and Ronald has, as ever, answered the call from his Surrey home, so they are free agents). Likewise, the ladies' team on the border will look sparse to anyone used to the crush of a welldressing in full production. Indeed, the fact that Jim has the time to dress instead of supervising and responding to calls for help and advice is an indication that the pressure is off. Incidentally, the separation of the sexes, which by this time has become more vestigial than customary, would have been even more apparent a few hours later.*

Clue 3. *The young onlookers are not at school so, as even Margaret would draw the line at welldre.ssing before 9 o'clock of a morning, it must be late afternoon at the earliest.*

Clue 4. *I confess, calls for a little research: the outline picture has to be matched to the photographic records, which is no big task since the search can be narrowed to two dates – Jim's first year as designer (1970) and the change of venue from the Old Hall Farm cartshed (which this is) to his garage at Arrowdale Farm. It is, in fact, the screen entitled The Anointing of David, featured in Chapter 2, so the answer is:*

Holywell workshop between 4.30 and 6.30pm on Tuesday, 21st June, 1977.

seen actually riding the bicycle: mostly he pushed it along with something or other on the handlebars; sometimes he just pushed it. He lived in a tiny cottage, from which his ancient wife sold household necessities like rubbing stone, aspirins and vinegar ... there's another thing, what happened to all those little shops – dozens there must have been – converted from unused parlours? Billy's cottage had a single living room with a large, whitewashed chimney-breast.

He would have been described in the euphemism of the time as *not much of a scholar* and, as is the way with those whose minds and memories are uncluttered by detritus of the written word, he had a perception of signs and symbols denied the rest of us. When a housewife called to ask for her chimney to be swept, he would study an array of incomprehensible-seeming marks on the chimney-breast and in his clipped business-voice, innocent of *double entendre* say *"Now then, missus, I can manage thee next Wednesday afternoon, if that'll suit thee."* And, with the arrangement confirmed, he would make a single crayon stroke on the chimney-breast that, to the casual eye, would look exactly like all the other strokes. Be that as it may, Billy was always there on time – and at the right house.

At the end of the year, when other people bought new desk diaries, l suppose Billy whitewashed his chimney-breast.

Chapter 4
INTEGRITY

Why do we dress the taps? Or to be more specific, for whom do we dress the *taps*? The question is an ethical quagmire and we are now on slippery ground. The notion that we might be dressing the taps for an audience borders on the obscene in the mind of at least one ardent welldresser I know and, for sure, there are others who may be of the same mind but less ready to expostulate it. *"Welldressing is an ancient custom"* is the admonition. *"not a tourist attraction"*.

I have no argument with that. The last thing any serious welldresser would wish is for the custom to become another artefact in the paraphernalia of *Interpretation* and *Folk Art* promoted and nurtured by the stewards of the national park we live in. Years ago, an old welldresser said to me *We would keep dressing the taps even if nobody came to see them.*. I think the sentiment is no less true today – at least, in villages where the custom is long-established – and the integrity of the tradition may well depend on it. What the purists fail to acknowledge is that visitors can be accommodated without compromising the principle; it is a matter of priorities My old welldresser friend was quite sincere in his contention but it did not prevent him from lingering by the screens at midsummer to bask secretly in the warmth of visitors' admiration.

Welldressing is not like the theatre that has no meaning without an audience. Welldressing exists as a celebration in itself. The attention of an audience is relevant, though incidental, and what the expectation of an audience must not do is to influence either the means or the end. I daresay there are villages for whom welldressing is a form of tourist promotion and, certainly. extramural welldressing events such as the recent exhibition at the Chatsworth Fair have no other purpose. But I know of no old-established festival that subjugates its principles to box-office interests. Rather more common is the venue where the welldressings have been tacked onto an existing function, such as a carnival. In these cases the quality of the welldressing tends to reflect the priorities of the organisers, almost as if the welldressers see themselves as queue entertainers.

At this point in history, I believe Youlgrave to be foremost in a welldressing eminence that derives from a long period of commitment and dedication to a single purpose. That is not to say that visitors are, or should be, neglected. Once the integrity of the tapdressing is assured, the prescription of hospitality alone requires that visitors are made welcome, provided for, comforted and informed to the best of our ability. Youlgrave's success has been in keeping the horse before the cart.

Margaret makes no bones about it; she is dressing for an audience.

"it is my strong belief, that for the most part the public like a familiar Bible story. it is also central to my thinking that, to be effective the picture needs to be bold and strong enough to make an impact at a distance as people approach it. I like best of all to choose a picture and portray it in such a way that the public with even a slender knowledge of the Bible can recognise it without the written title."

No sideshows! No competition! No commercialism! These are the three commandments of welldressing in Youlgrave and the visitors who come looking for any such diversion will be disappointed. Their interests are deemed incompatible. They may complain that other, equally-accredited welldressers have their fairs and fiestas, their carnivals and queens, their rivalries, their mild saturnalia. How does Youlgrave come to be so straightlaced about a spot of harmless merrymaking?

Well, the first thing that has to be said is that it is not unique. Other distinguished villages are similarly exclusive. Nor, surprisingly, is the abstinence traditional. It is a deliberate policy formulated and pursued over little more than forty years which, for all its strict adherence, could be changed overnight with no bones broken. Before that, Youlgrave could carouse with the best of them – the Club Feast, the Saturday-night dance, the Fair – and it was a case of necessity, not virtue, that put an end to them. By the 1960s, the Committee had decided that extraneous fund-raising events were no longer necessary, and this was the release that allowed the Youlgrave festival to develop in the way that it has. Intriguingly, it was the post-war influx of visitors that triggered the release, so the purists who maintain that the integrity of the custom should be protected from the influence of the visitors who made it possible are ignoring the facts of history. Here is how it came to be.

There was a time up until World War II, when welldressing was very much a local affair financed by local cash. It was not just the cost of overheads and materials that had to be met: the welldressers themselves had to be paid. At times the money would be provided by sponsors such as the Waterworks Committee and the Foresters and, when it was not, the custom itself was at risk of failing. In the early part of this century, it was financed by household subscriptions; two men were appointed each year, to visit every house in the village and ask for donations towards the forthcoming welldressing festival. The practice was abandoned in 1946.

Today, the entire expense of welldressing in Youlgrave is met from the donations that visitors place in the collecting boxes. In 1947 it represented 40%[1], the rest coming from pri-

---

[1] 50 years earlier, this percentage was an even less significant source of revenue. Coins left by visitors (and residents) were seen as *tips*.

vate donations, a raffle and the proceeds from a dance organ-ised and staffed by welldressers. There are now no distrac-tions: traffic control and car parking are in the hands of the parish council – as are the proceeds thereof – and the sale of souvenir photographs is left to the village shops. Welldressers today have but one purpose: to create and erect five welldress-ings by Midsummer Saturday morning before the streets are aired. They can then take to their beds for a few hours and know that nothing is spoiling.

Charity begins ... Of equal significance to the change that has come about in raising the money to dress wells has been the way in which it is spent. As Margaret mentioned earlier, it had been the long-established practice for surplus funds to be allo-cated to each Tap for distribution amongst the dressers accord-ing to a simple – but inequitable – sliding scale. In July 1952, the Committee debated a resolution that the share-out practice should cease and, in future, *"welldressings would be on a volun-tary basis"*. The resolution failed amidst some acrimony but it was not to be the end of it. Attitudes had been struck from which, no doubt, controversy simmered over the next few years until, in March 1956, the resurrected proposal was car-ried – significantly by unanimous agreement. The antagonists had left the field, supposedly resigning themselves to the inevitable. Rumour has it that some long-experienced well-dressers took umbrage, never again to press petal to clay.

The argument was not really about money. The old justifica-tion of possible hardship was no longer valid. It was about the principle and I suspect the principle concerned is a little more subtle than appears on the surface. As previously explained, welldressing was always men's business and the *breadwinner* had to be compensated for any loss of breadwinning potential. It was axiomatic. Then the order changed. The ladies were raising their profile – as a glance at the 1946 Minute Book plainly reveals. Welldressing was no longer a male dominion so the breadwinning imperative ceased to be valid.

I daresay the protagonists at the time would look somewhat askance at the fanciful theory of Youlgrave's amateur status hinging on the emancipation of women welldressers. Of course, it didn't. It was changing times and perceptions that banished the practice of divvying out the cash: the removal of a redundant argument merely anaesthetised the operation. Still it took ten years though its consequences were rather more instantaneous.

When virtue triumphs it acquires its own momentum. One step on the course of altruism is sure to be followed by another. Renouncing Mammon became a statement: *Welldressing is a religious festival from the purpose of which no distraction may be allowed.* Unspoken, unarticulated even, it nevertheless grew into a policy as austere, probably, as anything that had gone before. Biased I may be but, to me, without the dedication and coherence that it engendered, Youlgrave welldressings, for all the brilliance of the designers, could not have remained paramount for so long.

Income ... The three components of the austerity, mentioned above, will be analysed in a moment. First a couple of observations on the subject of money. The custom of welldressing has waxed and waned, village to village, generation to generation throughout history, and nobody knows the reason why. The waxing is even more inexplicable than the waning. All sorts of explanation have been offered, but I wonder ... does not the Youlgrave experience point to nothing more mysterious than the availability, or otherwise, of the wherewithal? If the welldressers of old were so constrained by what they could afford, periods of inactivity in the last century could well have coincided with the absence of sponsors and patrons. This would be particularly significant in leadmining villages such as Youlgrave whose fortunes were vulnerable to industrial vicissitudes; estate villages, on the other hand, would enjoy the patronage of the squire – and *captive welldressers* – hence their welldressing continuity would be assured and their records uninterrupted.

Lack of the wherewithal may explain the waning, but what about the waxing? Experience suggests that customs do not hibernate successfully: once asleep they tend to die. For all that, there is something very enduring about the welldressing tradition and spontaneous resurgence cannot be ruled out. The lesson from Youlgrave, however, is that it will tend to lie dormant indefinitely until some special event, such as the Waterworks inauguration, or the initiative of an individual or body like the Ancient Order of Foresters, provides the motivation and the cash to invigorate it.

Happily, the explanation now seems to be of academic importance. Welldressing everywhere can never have been so vigorous and one of the most influential reasons is surely the financial security provided by visitor numbers and their contributions. Those who worry about the impact of visitors should be more concerned for the effect of their absence than their presence.

... and expenditure ... Since visitors are providing the income they are entitled to know how it is spent. What, after 1956, did the welldressers do with the proceeds when they were no longer pocketing them? Therein lies another saga. Eventually, it was decided that, rather than run the risk of making fish and flesh in the village, all surplus funds should be allocated to a pre-designated national charity, identified by name on the collecting boxes and discreetly featured in the welldressing designs. The policy was short-lived. After a few smooth years, as is usually the case, somebody put a spoke in the wheel. It was pointed out to the Committee, possibly by a selected charity, that the law required a minimum of 75% of the proceeds to be handed on. The Committee took fright: it had become the practice to underline the significance of welldressing by making regular token donations to the religious houses and the Waterworks Committee. In a lean year. the arithmetic might not work out and the 75% minimum would be breached.

Youlgrave Welldressing Committee nevertheless retained its

charitable status and the policy is the same now as it has been for the past twenty-odd years. Any excess of income over expenditure is put in a deposit account and allowed to accumulate. When the balance becomes substantial the Committee looks round for a project that *will benefit the village as a whole*. That way, no-one can grumble about favouritism. It is a slow process. With new boards costing up to £800 and the mounting expense of materials, the margin between income and expenditure is sometimes too close for comfort.

The downside ... The virtuous policy post–1956 – *Welldressing is a religious festival from which no distraction is allowed* – contained an intrinsic paradox. It envisioned a simple celebration in which visitors, devout or not, should feel themselves to be a part. Perhaps less nobly conceived was the anxiety that the new spirit of voluntary togetherness might prove fragile were others seen to be exploiting it. It is one thing to propose a simple *thanksgiving celebration*, quite another to realise and sustain it. Welldressings attract large crowds of people, and large crowds of people attract other people eager to profit their own enterprise. They mostly – not always – have money in mind. It is difficult, for instance, to engender an atmosphere of quiet dedication when some icecream vendor parks his van where the Blessing takes place and peddles his wares with engine running throughout the Service. Likewise, a newsboy loudly touting his pages on the streets of Youlgrave is an alien enough sight in itself; it becomes even more unwelcome when the product turns out to be a souvenir edition of somebody else's welldressing.

The three negatives – no sideshows, no competition, no commercialism – are, just that ... negatives, and a negative attitude seems to be incompatible with the concept of thanksgiving. What is more, prohibition and goodwill are not usually mutual companions. Yet in the absence of street authority, goodwill was all the Welldressing Committee could summon to impose their philosophy. A little blood was shed but persis-

THE TAP DRESSERS: A CELEBRATION

tence paid; people came to recognise that tranquillity can be as relevant to welldressing as to a walk in the woods. All it needed was an eagle eye, a thick skin and a finger to stick in the dyke.

No sideshows ... Why not? It is a festival, after all, and where is the festival without the fair? I suppose the answer must be that priorities have changed. In years gone by, public holidays were cherished for their rarity and for their relief from monotony. Old customs – including Christmas and Shrove Tuesday – were as eagerly observed for the comfort and self-indulgence they provided as for the meaning they conveyed. Nowadays most people have all the comfort they need and self-indulgence is a mere matter of taste and inclination. So what happens? They yearn for the *simple life of yesteryear* and seek spiritual fulfilment (who is yet to deplore the can't-wait commercialism of Christmas?). Youlgrave welldressers believe – and other villages have come to the same conclusion – that the aesthetic simplicity of a welldressing festival carries a special appeal in a world dominated by rampant consumerism.

There is another consideration, perhaps less virtuously based: job satisfaction is a great motivator and the jobber is never so satisfied as when his work is the centre of interest.

But like all abstract concepts, the formulation is a good deal easier than the implementation. How, for instance, do you explain to a band of dedicated Morris Dancers, who have turned up uninvited to bring lustre to the festival that their joyous cavorting might be historically better suited to a revel than to a Christian thanksgiving ceremony? And what can you say to a visiting evangelist who hires strategically-placed premises to cream off a congregation for his welldressing roadshow?

Intolerance of another kind of sideshow is even more difficult to justify, yet equally – if not more – imprudent to overlook. From time to time, this or that group of children has produced and displayed their own welldressing – usually with an invitation to leave a small token of appreciation in a good cause. The Committee as long ago as June 1931 recorded what reads like a long-suffering resolution to *"stop children from making their own welldressings"*. Surely, none but a curmudgeon would deny so innocent an enterprise. Possibly not, though the curmudgeons of 1931 clearly thought it necessary as have their successors over the next three generations. Forget the implication of syphoned funds, there are two issues of principle at stake. Firstly, the product of these youthful endeavours has rarely been more than a crude imitation: embarrassing, if only by association, to a village that prides itself on the quality of its screens. More importantly, the Youlgrave structure of five self-contained units is only viable if continuity over the complete age-range is maintained by means of recruitment and attachment at a tender age. The careers of the Youlgrave designers testify to the fact that there are only five places in the village where a good welldressing education begins and where a durable commitment to welldressing is more-or-less assured. Though the village school is not one of them, its authority has more than once proved a decisive instrument for redirecting youthful enthusiasm.

No competition ... Several idiosyncracies could illustrate Youlgrave's aversion to competition: one will suffice. When the Treasurer empties the boxes of the donations that visitors have kindly left in appreciation of each screen, he must put the proceeds into one bag and count it in total. He may not reveal the amounts in each box since it might be inferred that this Tap had done better than that and, by inference, one Tap *had won*. Why when other villages seem to thrive on rivalry should Youlgrave so fervently abjure it?

The simplest answer is that it cannot do otherwise if it hopes to preserve its integrity in the role it has set for itself as a simple thanksgiving for water. How can a celebrant be a *loser*? Aspiring to be the best welldressing team is appropriate only if the end-product is the end in itself. And who – in all modesty – is qualified to judge the Youlgrave screens?

There is, in fact, one very good reason why competition is inimical to the Youlgrave ethos. Each screen is the product of a specialised team – *specialised* in the sense that it has developed its own style over many years – and there are no common standards by which to compare them. I suppose it would be possible to rate them in a negative sort of way – marks off for shortcuts, inaccurate petalling and the like – but what purpose it would serve is hard to see. No, the great strength of the Youlgrave tradition is that there is no common denominator; each screen is a different experience and for casual visitor and connoisseur alike that can only add spice to life. Why sacrifice it for an incentive without credentials ?

No commercialism ... Perhaps *no wishful thinking* should also be the rule. Some buying and selling is bound to occur, if only to serve the needs of visitors, and bearing in mind the contribution that voluntary fund-raising makes to the vitality of village life, the Welldressing Committee would be singularly self-centred if it tried to suppress it.

The complication comes when non-village organisations come with their fund-raising, peripatetic traders who, so convinced of their own worthy cause, will find it reprehensible to be denied the chance of turning a charitable penny on the back of someone else's. Alas, one market stall looks much like another and this year's worthy vendor of wildlife tea-towels may be next year's plant and pottery pedlar.

The aspiration of the welldressers – and in the absence of any direct authority it can only be an *aspiration* – is that, if there is money to be made incidentally from their endeavours, it should be, firstly, to the benefit of the village's voluntary organisations and, secondly, to those local businesses that serve the village throughout the year.

For once the traffic problem is on our side. The combination of crowded streets and an inhospitable reception must have long since persuaded the traders that their time would be better spent elsewhere. With luck, the hostile reputation that Youlgrave had to struggle to acquire will be good for a few more years to come.

About dates ... For a welldressing fraternity with an above-average conviction on most other things to do with their art, a year-after-year palaver about the proper date for the festival seems oddly out-of-character. It has been no less a fact of life for all that. Hopefully, there is no longer any cause for confusion, always provided everyone understands the rules. So here, as much for the benefit of the village as for visitors, is a step-by-step rationale to settle future arguments:

Principle 1: The first thing to remember is that Midsummer Day is the key date. That said, we are straight into the kind of dispute that the explanation is meant to avert. When is Midsummer Day? Some say the 21st June, others say the 24th. Whatever may be the case in the rest of the nation, Midsummer in Youlgrave falls on the 24th June. The 21st June is the summer solstice, about which there can be no possible argument, although it is as well not to question how a season that supposedly begins on one day reaches its mid-point three days later.

Why is the 24th June so important? As we profess to being a Christian festival, I am bound to claim it commemorates the feast of St. John the Baptist which falls on that date, St John being the patron saint of water. Despite that, there is the strong suspicion that it might have pagan credentials. Christmas and Easter are just two examples of Christian celebrations being grafted on to pagan feasts so as to cause least impediment to religious conversion. Perhaps St. John merely took over some earlier bacchanalian appointment, but no matter, it is the date not its provenance that we have to remember.

Principle 2: The second thing, to remember is that the festival must begin on a Saturday – and there lies the crux of past argument. Unlike, say, Ascension Day, which always falls on a Thursday, Midsummer Day trawls through all the days of the week, so which is the appropriate Saturday if none happens to be the 24th?

For many years Youlgrave shared the same rule-of-thumb as several other villages: the Saturday nearest to Midsummer was deemed to be the effective date. Problem solved ... not quite. If 24th June is a Wednesday, the Saturday either side would qualify, and that ambiguity is the reason why one of the most portentous items of Committee business, year-by-year, was *to fix the date of next year's festival*. A variety of prescriptions were tried until someone had the perception to see that it was the date, not the day, when the screens had to be in place. Hence the Saturday on or preceding the 24th was always the appropriate day to start the festival ... simple ... problem solved ... not quite! What happens if the 24th is a Friday – a non-day for Youlgrave? There has to be a rider, after all. Everybody will have to remember that when the 24th June is a Friday the Welldressings will start next day.

And there lies the explanation, for those who may have wondered, why Youlgrave seems occasionally to get *out of sync* with the other festivals with which it has historically coincided. It is not Youlgrave that gets *out of sync*, it is the rest of the world.

Principle 3: Although the ceremony of welldressing is confined to the Saturday, it remains as a spectacle for the next five days. The screens are always in place and inevitably at their pristine best early on Saturday morning and, whatever their condition, they are relentlessly broken up the following Friday teatime. Nothing is left to chance: all possible channels of communication are mobilised to tell the world that the Youlgrave festival ends on Thursday.

And the chances are that, within an hour of Friday's demolition, at least one coachload of sightseers will be cruising through the village looking for welldressings.

Chapter 5

CHANGING WITH THE TIMES

The first reaction of most people on their introduction to a welldressing screen is astonishment and admiration; the second is to wonder whether it can last – the custom, that is, not the screen. The doubt is understandable; it must appear as some quaint remnant of a vanished age that will inevitably succumb to *progress*. Things of the past have no future in our millennial society.

We should not be too pessimistic. The resilience of welldressing is apparent to anyone with a memory long enough to judge. It may appear to be set in a time warp but it has both changed and endured change: *changed* because techniques, even the shape of the screens themselves, have responded to progressive thinking; endured change because it has accommodated the demands of modem society – traffic, visitors needs and convenience, fluctuating resources (both human and financial) and pressure to exploit it. *Can it survive?* We can only consider the evidence.

Changing streets ... Picture the street-scene when all the tapspots were in daily use, little more than fifty years ago. There is the occasional vehicle to be sure, but it is more a thoroughfare for pedestrians and livestock. As for the schoolchild-

ren, this is where they safely dribble their footballs, pig's blad-
ders, tin cans or pebbles, in that order of preference; where,
according to season, they play hopscotch, shoot marbles, skim
cigarette cards, bowl hoops[1], scurry after spinning tops and
wind-sped whirligigs, teeter on stilts or captive cocoa tins, pro-
pel themselves on home-made trolleys, rollerskates and scoot-
ers and in between, whirl sparking touchwood burners round
their heads. No child ever went straight to school and back
other than for reasons beyond his control. In winter, while the
snow lay compacted on the street, boys would be *sledging bel-
lyflop* (toboganning prone) until well after dark[2]. But for the
most part parents had good reason to dispatch their children
out-of-doors with a lack of concern that would earn them a
visit from a social worker today.

It was a time when people met and talked in mid-street,
standing aside briefly now and again before returning to their
first point of contact. They could usually count on several minutes of animated conversation without interruption.

*   *   *   *   *   *

---

[1] Called *bowls* to rhyme with *howls,* they were made from 5/16th inch mild
steel rod and formed *while-you-wait* by Johnny Walker, the village black-
smith, into a precise hoop about 30 inches in diameter, together with a short
rod with a hook on the business end for control of speed and direction; they
were propelled with a panache and dexterity reminiscent of the skateboards
that, years later, served a similar function. Less well-equipped children
made do with a tyre-less bicycle wheel and a wooden baton. All were
securely parked in the cloakroom during schooltime; ownership was sacrosanct and *joybowling* a moral sin.

[2] On second thoughts, perhaps I should remember that '*safely*' label; the
memory springs too readily to mind of a sledge disappearing under the
front axle of Mr Curtis's trundling hardware/paraffin cart and emerging
unscathed from the rear end. The rider must remain anonymous since,
against all the odds, he is alive today – more than can be said for the kindly
Mr Curtis whose lifespan must have been foreshortened by such traumas in
the service of the community.

One Saturday morning, Billy was sweeping the chimney to a sizeable house on Main Street, beginning as always with the flue brush being thrust up the chimney by rods connected in series. Not being sure how many rods it would take, he asked an obliging passer-by to stand in the street and call to him when the flue brush emerged from the chimney. So it began with Billy indoors connecting the rods and pushing them up the chimney and the chance-assistant keeping watch in the street. It was not to last. Soon, a third party came along and chatted briefly to the brush-spotter before, Billy forgotten, they both wandered off down the street. The flue-brush emerged from the chimney, was soon noticed and, by the time it had crept jerkily down the roof, past the bedroom window and into the street below. a small crowd had gathered to watch and wonder. Billy, having run out of rods for the first time in his memory, emerged from the house in a proper mucksweat, looked at the spectators, looked at the dangling brush, lifted his hat, scratched his head and said *"Sithee, 'e never let on"*, which was Billy's way of saying *he might at least have sent me a postcard.*

*   *   *   *   *   *

What can't be cured ... it could hardly happen today, if only because pedestrians dodging vehicles are unlikely to notice errant flue-brushes. Remorseless traffic threading in and out of cars parked nose to tail, children being ferried to and from school by anxious mothers, ancient walls scraped by clandestine[3] trucks. Had the internal combustion engine preceded the welldressing custom, the chances of the latter ever taking root here have to be reckoned extremely slim. Youlgrave was never equipped for the horseless carriage and it is little comfort to know that it shares this incompatibility with almost all the old leadmining villages. They were built when there were more

---

[3] The road through the village is legally weight-restricted.

cobblers than engine fitters and the nearest thing to a garage was a stable. The village that once was off the beaten track is off the beaten track no longer: as Ruskin might have said, all the *fools* on the A515 want to be on the A6 and all the *fools* on the A6 want to be on the A515. Youlgrave is in the way.

The ideal welldressing village has a pretty face, a handy car park, an open compact, traffic-free core and screens within easy reach of everyone, especially the disabled and infirm. An ideal welldressing village is what Youlgrave most definitely is not and it casts longing eyes on the facilities of those that are.

... must be patiently endured. Well, not altogether patiently endured. The welldressings have adapted to change. Three screens have been moved to less hazardous locations, the Saturday afternoon *Service* has been moved to the less-congested *Holywell* from its traditional site at *The Fountain*, during which traffic through the village is halted by the police. Temporary car parks are provided by the parish council at each end of the village and street traders are banished. Arrangements are made for the setting-down and picking-up of coach passengers. Pedestrians can safely stand back and view each screen, either directly or through the viewfinder of a camera, with the limited exception of *Bank Top*.

All of which, it will be quite justifiably argued, are merely cosmetic changes. Where is the evidence that the welldressings themselves have adapted to survive the onslaught. There is none, of course, but there is evidence of triumph in adversity, so to speak. It may only be coincident that Youlgrave's screens have got better as the traffic has got worse: it may be impertinent to say that villages happily free of the problem seem to be correspondingly indifferent to standards. It matters not; a major impediment of *progress* has been surmounted and, who knows, one day more coach drivers may be encouraged to stop their vehicles long enough for the passengers to get out.

*   *   *   *   *   *

The changing screen ... Part of the so called *mystery of a well-dressing* is its apparent timelessness. It endures like a stained glass window, unchanging, its origins lost in history, its nature untouched by the passage of time. This is a misconception. Records reveal a major change in the shape and size of the screen. The picture has progressed from relative insignificance to dominance during the century we are about to leave and the changes have come about largely as a result of designers seeking new opportunities for artistic expression. Some changes have come about for practical reasons. When a set of boards reaches the end of its working life[4], the designer may take the opportunity to try something different. Perhaps a bigger board if the team are feeling energetic, or a smaller one if not[5]. It may be an opportunity to overcome some difficulty with assembly or just an opportunity for the designer and his team to try something more – or less – adventurous

Since most people viewing a work of art do not spend too much time studying the frame, the structural alterations to the Youlgrave screens may have passed unnoticed. What may have a much deeper significance than the construction is the evolution of the screen in relation to its setting.

The photograph of Bank Top in 1903 reveals a screen that was relatively subordinate to the garlands that surrounded it. This relationship existed at all the Taps up to this century and the garland was still a prominent feature right up to the 1930s; at the same time the picture screen was becoming pro-

---

[4] A set of boards will last as long as the team are prepared to keep cobbling it together. After eight years it is probably beyond repair.

[5] Assembling a set of dressed boards is a delicate operation that becomes more hazardous with each pound in weight. The Coldwell picture board is probably the heaviest at around 2cwts. with another 6 cwts. in the surround.

gressively more dominant[6]. I have seen a photograph of a huge greenery garland that spanned the main street and provided a *gateway* to *The Fountain*. The prominence of this one-time practice leads me to believe that, if we had the benefit of photographic records reaching back in time, we would eventually arrive at a point where only the garland remained and we, in You}grave, would be sharing, with Europe a common form of tribute to whatever God or gods were held sovereign at the time. Those who were privileged to see the festival in Erbach found evidence enough to reinforce this view. As can be plainly seen, the garland still persists in vestigial form, like the human coccyx. No welldressing is complete without its proxy garland of fir trees[7].

The streets of Youlgrave are austere. There are no ornate bowers no greenswards to enhance the setting. One of Fred's guest dressers made a very handsome flower trough that softens the transition from blossom to tarmac. Margaret experimented with a stone water trough at the foot of her screen that was admired by everyone except the Treasurer, who nightly, had the job of fishing out coins from the elbow-deep water and transferring them to the collecting box where they should have been. It must be said that neither device can be classified as a significant advance in welldressing presentation.

One innovation that was most certainly significant was the introduction of floodlighting in 1953. Not only does it cancel out Youlgrave's main disadvantage by enabling the screens to be viewed in the comparative traffic-free serenity of late

---

[6] It is difficult to generalise: the rate of change varied from tap to tap. The Reading Room and Fountain became the avant garde whose predominance was also recognised in preferential practices such as the distribution of proceeds and places on the committee. By the turn of this century, they had already developed the familiar board design and dimensions of today, thanks largely to the individual influences described later.

[7] Conservationists need not despair: these are thinnings from commercial woods.

evening, it also provides an aesthetic dimension of its own that, regrettably, so few visitors seem aware of.

Can welldressing innovation advance even further without offending traditional parameters and the viewers' perception of them? Or, indeed, does it need to? Are a flat profile and a border picture format sacrosanct and inviolable? A welldresser who shall be nameless once told me of his scheme for a cylindrical screen mounted on an electrically-propelled turntable and rotating to reveal an unfolding scenario – perfectly feasible in these technological times. Is it such an outlandish idea? As pointed out in Appendix II, the screen at *The Fountain* in 1894 incorporated a moving feature. Far from being scandalised, the village applauded, so the reason why it was not repeated must be a matter of practice rather than principle. Well, it may not be an idea for serious consideration, but what a leap in welldressing development that would be!

Changing people ... For as long as nature continues to provide the materials the state of health of the welldressing custom hangs as it always has, on the question of resources. The last fifty years have been a tonic in terms of *financial resources.* Are we entitled to feel as optimistic about the human resources – the willing welldressers? Again, we must consider the evidence.

The people who dressed the wells sixty-odd years ago were countrymen. Their lifestyle, the way they associated, their horizons and their prospects were quite distinct from those of the townsmen. For the first third of the century Youlgrave had no gas, the older houses were lit by paraffin lamps, indoor plumbing was basic at best and an open range provided the cooking and hot water. It was a relatively static society. Personal transport was sparse and few people travelled far beyond the range of the local bus service or their own legs. Social activities were mostly home-made and centred around the chapels, the village hall and the Reading Room: the community was closely integrated. It was a way of life that the more adventurous townsmen such as ramblers and cyclists liked to sample in small doses but had no wish to embrace on a more regular basis.

Anonymity was impossible. People lived up – or down – to what was expected of them. It was a combination of pride and obligation that came to be known as the *village spirit.* Welldressing was a major component of the village spirit in Youlgrave and the village spirit was a major stimulus to well-dressing.

It is a much different village today. Interdependence has gone: people go their own way without too much regard for what is expected of them. Personal mobility, either to make journeys or to move home, is the prerogative of individuals and their families. Homes are serviced and appointed with every comfort, television and computers keep them self-contained. With rural living now no longer synonymous with hardship, people come and go at will and the social structure and coherence of the village has altered. We are no longer countrymen.

So why are we still dressing the *taps*? This past fifty years of comparative comfort and affluence have seen perhaps the most prolonged and concentrated-ever period of welldressing activity here and in other villages. Why, if the village spirit was distilled from the shared tribulation of the old orefields, has it not evaporated in the economic sunshine?

There are two reasons: firstly, the demise of the village spirit is a superficial perception. Local people[8] may be less in touch with each other but they are no less in touch with the past. There is a social print-through as deeply embedded in the village awareness as the watermark in a banknote. It is ineradicable. It is a state of *belonging* without which a village community would have no more character than a high-rise tower block

---

[8] A few years ago, the local authority conducted a survey into what comprised a *local person*. A popular answer was *three generations in the churchyard.*

and without which even the most thriving community enterprise is in danger of becoming a passing phase.

Nevertheless, it has no function of its own other than to provide a sense of *belonging* and shared nostalgia: it may infuse an
extant institution but it cannot provide one. The vigour of
welldressing owes much to the dedication of people who have
no ancestral roots, the *incomers* for want of a softer expression.
This is the second reason why the change in the village character has brought about, not a a decline, but an invigoration of
village activities. They have come to live here from choice, not
because they like what they see and are anxious to preserve it.
Their well dressing may not be impelled by the religious and
communal obligations of old but it makes good cause with
those who have gone before. It is a little ironic that the growth
of materialism that has brought such change to society should
itself generate a vaccine to sustain a tradition that could hardly
be more benevolent. It bodes well for the future, but Youlgrave
may not fare so well as some of its more easterly neighbours
should material prosperity come to be the criterion of welldressing vigour.

The signs – or almost all of them – are that the social and
demographic changes of these last fifty years point to a very
secure future. There is one small cloud on the horizon: the next
generation – or the one after that – or the one after that. Fifty
years ago, the formative years of most young people from
childhood to adulthood was circumscribed by the village.
Throughout this period they were under the influence of the
local school, not just for the time they were in the classroom
but for their leisure hours too. Headmasters like G.W. Gimber,
and Harold Lees lived in the village and were a commanding
presence in the community. They were prominent welldressers
who encouraged their charges to take an interest. Both were
designers whose wives supported them, as Ruth recalls: *"I
have always been involved with dressing the same well and started
doing so under the supervision of Mrs Lees – as most people of my
generation did."*

Today, at eleven years of age and on the brink of graduating from flower collecting to dressing, the children transfer to Lady Manners Comprehensive School in Bakewell and continuity is lost. The shortage of young welldressers is now giving the designers some cause for concern and the Committee has made approaches to the local school. Unfortunately, they are having to address the wrong school population.

The dilemma finds its echo in another celebrated Youlgrave enterprise. The annual pantomime first appeared in 1929/31 and was re-introduced to raise funds for the village hall in 1962. It quickly gained renown throughout the district and runs to packed houses for 12 performances each January/ February and, as can be expected with this kind of fame, there is no shortage of would-be performers. There is one exception: In 1962 there were enough young adults to provide two separate choruses; now there are none. The children at Youlgrave school scramble to be auditioned. But when they move on to Bakewell they form new associations and interests, their lives are regimented by homework and examinations and, if they embark on higher education, they lose all but family connections. The pantomime's reputation ensures that it does not have to rely on home-grown talent for its cast list; continuity is lost with regret but with no dire consequences.

Alas, welldressing is less favourably placed.

So the answer to the question is *yes, welldressing will last – so long as there are people willing to do it*. The custom has weathered dramatic social change during this century and has emerged stronger than ever, but there is a significant divergence. Whereas in a village such as Youlgrave there was a kind of tribal obligation, dressing the *taps* is now a matter of personal fulfilment for a growing number. At times in the past when the welldressing custom fell dormant for some reason, it could lie for decades like a poppy seed in the soil of village identity, ready to reappear when conditions were right. Is the soil still there?

Youlgrave looks set for the next Millennium. Perhaps the

time will come when it can no longer dress five *taps* – a demanding programme for a comparatively small village – but I for one, am confident that welldressing will have a Youlgrave dimension for generations yet to come. I am less confident that, should it fall into abeyance for any reason, it will spring back to life so readily for our descendants as it did for our forbears.

*   *   *   *   *   *

Of the following photographs, the first three – covering a three-generation at Bank Top – illustrate conventional development. The fourth (Holywell) is an experimental concept that, had it caught on, might have changed the whole approach to welldressing presentation. The other three are as much about people as design.

1. Bank Top 1903

The dressing in its original site with the Washcroft in the background; the screen is relatively small and primitive.

2. Bank Top 1928

By 1928, it has moved across the road to its present site. The garland is identical to that 25 years previously but a dressed surround has been added and will eventually banish the garland. It was an innovation of relatively brief popularity.

3. Bank Top 1966

The 1966 illustration features the supporters to the border that were added in 1955, an appearance that, save for the addition of a floor-level flower box, has remained unchanged. The foliage has receded and now plays a very minor role in the presentation.

93

4. Holywell 1960

The screen has several interesting and distinctive features. The dressed outer surround, earlier seen at Bank Top, was still in use and would continue for another two years. The most notable feature is the offset side panels behind which the centreboard is set to simulate depth. Sometimes, as here, it was used to complement the main theme; the previous year it had been integrated with the main picture to produce a striking 3-D effect; the following year, it was used to portray the picture as if seen through a casement window. It was a unique innovation that lasted from 1958 to 1963 during the joint designership of Roger Bacon and Fred Billinge. Note the use of black-knobs for lining the picture, combined with henbeans in the border. The Ark was made entirely of henbeans, over which there were some misgivings; it was feared that the combined weight might overcome the clay adhesion and, even, that marauding birds might discover it. The instant rockery in the foreground was a presentation-aid that, not unsurprisingly, was abandoned from 1970 onwards. It persisted for longer at Bank Top.

95

5. Reading Room

This 1902 screen was the last designed at the Reading Room by Edwin Shimwell (standing on the left of the picture). As Messrs. J. W. & D. W Shimwell have pointed out, the board shape and construction has a particular signifcance in that, much in evidence elsewhere today, it provides an indication of those villages where the introduction of the custom owed much to the pioneering influence of Edwin and, later, his son Oliver. Although nowadays it may seem commonplace, the pilaster-effect of the side boards, surmounted by corbels and a canopied headboard were an outstanding innovation for the time. There is one small enigma: the prominent keyhole caps on each side of the headboard that are almost a Shimwell trademark in other villages (see The Church illustration) are not there. In fact, they were introduced by Samuel Nuttall a year or two later, but Edwin must clearly have taken a liking to them before he embarked on his travels. Conspicuously missing too, it will be noted, is any feminine presence. Though she may well regret the sexist implications, Ruth will surely look with envy on the size of the team.

96

6 The Fountain

How much of this 1908 Fountain board owes its design to Edwin (seen this time on the right) is not recorded The style and features up to canopy level are very similar to the Reading Room; the very unusual saw-tooth line above was not, nor did it survive. Sometime between 1920 and 1927, the Tap had to replace their board, thereby giving Edwin the chance to revert to the (now familiar) Reading Room design.

7 Bank Top

Budding Welldressers? Mainly not, as it happened, although one notable exception in this 1927 Bank Top photograph was a very young Freddie Shimwell. For the record, to save Youlgrave headscratching, the group comprises: From left back to front – Lilian Bacon, P. Birds, Kathleen Harrison, Grace Taylor, Mena Harrison, E. Shimwell, Ben Shimwell, Jim Frost, Dorothy Harrison, Freda Harrison (all sisters), A. Shimwell, G. Oldfeld, V. Bacon, Raymond Bird and himself.

Chapter 6
BRUNNENSCHMÜCKEREN

The Youlgrave Welldressing Committee is as gregarious as a hermit. Down the years it has politely declined all invitations to mount exhibitions elsewhere, to become involved in collective promotion or to associate with other welldressing villages. Although this may look seriously like a village-with-an-attitude, there is a rationale that saves it from the obvious accusation: Youlgrave Welldressings is a religious festival whose physical roots are considered to be inseparable from its character. If it becomes a transportable commodity or an end-product in itself, it loses its intrinsic meaning and, sooner or later, commercial imperatives come into the reckoning.

Considering that, for the last sixty years and beyond, Youlgrave designers have been largely instrumental in the growth of the custom elsewhere[1] *ambivalent* might seem to be a generous description, but it is not as contrary as may appear. In fact, it accords very closely with the long-established infrastructure of self-contained, autonomous teams led by freelance, incumbent designers. What they get up to either side of Midsummer is entirely their own affair; the Committee is not

[1] See next chapter.

involved. And by that principle – some might say device – the individual practitioners of Youlgrave have sallied forth from time to time.

One such expedition is worth relating for a variety of reasons, the principal being it was an adventure, it tells us something about the nature and mystique of welldressing and, for those with innovation in mind, it is by way of being a *Beginners Guide to Welldressing.*

Overtures ... Thirty years ago, Derbyshire County Council was twinned with the Regierung of Hesse-Darmstädt in Germany through the British Council. A Regierung is an administrative area rather grander than an English county – more like the regions we are promised – with considerably more in the way of autonomy and population (5^1/$_2$ million). The former State of Hessen, once ruled by princes, one of whom married a daughter of Queen Victoria, was divided into two Regierungen, the southernmost of which is Hesse-Darmstädt. It is bounded by the Rhine, Main and Neckar rivers and was flanked in the north-east corner, in those days, by the wire of the German Democratic Republic. Before the formal links with the County of Derbyshire ended in 1976 – nothing to do, I hasten to add, with the events I am about to relate – a good rapport had been built between the two administrations both of whom were alert to opportunities for cultural exchange as the means to further international accord.

In October 1969, I was asked in the course of a casual conversation at County Hall whether I knew anyone in welldressing circles who might be prepared to organise a mission to Erbach-im-Odenwald the following May, there to dress two wells (English-fashion) for a special festival. I blinked and said I would give it some thought, the first of which was that the question could have been better phrased ... *did I know any crazy welldressers?* for instance. I suppose the answer to that was, yes, I do. There were, after all, those eager bands of *nouveau* welldressers about the County who, in the manner of St. Paul,

103

had come lately to the faith and were agog to share their expertise with the unenlightened in distant places. One of those might be fired up with enough momentum to clear all the insuperable hurdles in a single bound of enthusiasm. The idea lingered for as long as it took me to remember that the person usually held to blame for a debacle is the one who encouraged it. There the matter might have ended had I not been held, a few days later, to my promise to *give it some thought.*

I should explain that I knew Erbach from a brief visit two years earlier and I knew that only the best would do[2]. There was more at stake than the art of welldressing – or indeed Anglo-German solidarity, itself. No less than the honour, prestige and dignity of this ancient town would be resting on the success or failure of such an enterprise for reasons that will become clear as we go along. As to the best in welldressing, there were in my book but two contenders: Fred and Margaret were welldressing designers unsurpassed in Derbyshire (effectively the world) and if only they ... I was still thinking about it.

It was, first and foremost, a problem of logisitics and timespan: the welldressing process in Youlgrave has a lead-time of 52 weeks, beginning when the clay used for one year's festival is immediately replaced and put to soak for the next. By the beginning of the calendar year, the designers are planning and drawing their designs. In April/May the Committee turn their attention to routine preparations for the Service and procession – publicity, insurance, arrangements with the police and parish council for visitor and traffic management – and technical details such as floodlighting and Service sheets. The boards are taken out of store in early June and put in the river to soak. Ten days later, they are taken out and clad in clay ready for

---

[2] It was from the Darmstädter Echo report of 15th May (see illustration) that I discovered this opinion had already been pre-empted.

five days of concentrated well dressing. *Question one*: how could all this activity be packed into the eight-day invitation? *Question two*: what would the expedition do for boards, clay and materials, assuming that the travel arrangements would involve something a little more comfortable and urgent than a pick-up truck. *Question three*: what natural materials would be available, bearing in mind that both the local flora and the intended dates were ahead of the average season by some six weeks? *Question four*: remembering that language differences had put paid to the relatively simple task of constructing the Tower of Babel, how could anything as complicated as a well-dressing be accomplished without a common tongue? *Question five*: how could a small party of eight or so, do the work normally done by thirty?[3] Questions six, seven and eight there were, I am sure, but that seemed to be enough to be going on with. Both commonsense and instinct proclaimed it a non-starter and, in conscience, all I needed was confirmation from the experts. No doubt I would get it.

Hooked ... But I did not. Margaret was quite taken with the idea, Fred exhibited the kind of caution he reserves for projects already mentally classed as feasible, and the corner I was painting myself into began to contract.

But what, it may well be asked, did I perceive to be so special about a smallish town in distant Odenwald that it should command a connoisseurial introduction to welldressing? The answer, I suppose, was an abundance of civic pride, but more of that in a moment. First the Odenwald, itself, for those not privileged to have been there. It is, as I imagine the Black Forest before the tourists and confectioners took over, a landscape of hills and forests where legends and fairies abound,

---

[3] This was not a mutually-recognised problem, had I but known it, the would-be hosts envisaged an enterprise similar in scale and complexity to their own version of welldressing, a misapprehension that awaited its own dramatic dawn of understanding.

where the people are *Odenwalders* first and Germans second and where custom and folk-lore still flourish. Here rode the hunters of Charlemagne and the heroes of the Nibelungenglied; and here, but a few kilometres from Erbach, is the spring where Siegfried paused for refreshment and was slain by Hagan as he drank. Clearly, a natural ambience for welldressers.

Erbach, for all its size – or lack of it – I remembered as rich in civic and historic amenities. It had a castle, a famous Elfenbein (Ivory) Museum, a prize-winning brewery (of course), two potteries (for which heaven be praised!) and a festival hall of some magnificence. It was at the time famous – or perhaps in deference to today's international mores I should say *infamous* – as the Europe-wide centre of ivory-carving. Much more appealing to *Green* sensitivities – it had a celebrated folk-dance group, the Hans von der Au, that had performed throughout Europe and, later, came to charm the people of Derbyshire.

The town (*Kreisstadt*) is described in the guidebooks as a *Luftspa,* that it is to say a place to which people resort for the quality of its air rather than its water, notwithstanding the existence of several ancient wells. How it came to have a municipal distinction out of all proportion to its size is probably best explained by its unflagging determination to upstage its near-neighbour, Michelstadt, in all matters of civic pride. Hence in welldressing, as in all other matters of public endeavour, I knew that only the best would do for Erbach.

And *the best* were not saying No. Fred and Margaret were on *amber* and *green,* so I sought out Jim – level-headed, logical Jim, whose organising reputation as Secretary of the Youlgrave festival relied on his ability to anticipate snags. He would be the arbiter of feasibility. His version of a cautious response was to sign up immediately for a crash-course in German-speaking and, having thus acquired a chief of staff and back-up designer at a stroke, I had run out of legs to stand on. County Hall were duly advised that the project could be upgraded from *impossi-*

ble to *improbable* and that all that stood in the way of a successful venture were a few insuperable problems.

Excursions ... So the Regierung were informed and the ball began to roll. Welldressers with experience of displaying their art away from home will know that the easiest option, logistically speaking, is to dress the screen in-house and transport it complete to its destination. The safest – and in our case *only* – option, was to dress on-site, which called for a measure of advance planning and coordination. For this we would perforce rely on our German hosts, so the final pre-commitment ploy was to seek confirmation that it would be forthcoming. Would-be welldressers with d-i-y propensities may find the following list useful (the only justification for reproducing it in full), which was despatched to the Regierung – via the translators, of course. Why admit the risk of misunderstanding to an already ticklish situation? Why, indeed?

Materials requirement per Welldressing:
1. Well-lit spacious and covered working area, trestles to carry screen boards during horizontal dressing, temporary seating and hessian covers for overnight protection during dressing.
2. Wooden screens similar in size and design to the enclosed sketch (Working drawings to be supplied).
3. Approximately 160 kilograms of malleable clay.
4. A supply of flower heads, lichen, parsley, etc. in accordance with a more detailed list to follow.
5. At least 2 young spruce trees to form a surround, and foliage for a decorative foreground.
6. Picket posts and ropes to provide a public barrier.
7. A ground-mounted floodlight.

Working Team per Welldressing
From Youlgrave:
1 A designer to select subject, design picture and

borders, prepare templates and estimate material requirements.

2. In addition, a cadre of at least three experienced welldressers.

From Erbach:

1. At least 6 local volunteers (spare time) to assist with dressing under instruction - of necessity, one English-speaking.

2. Two or three "scouts" (possibly children) to forage for materials and run errands

3 . Staff to arrange all matters of ceremony, publicity, sale of photographs and souvenirs.

No problem, we were assured. The reply was as positive as the speed at which it was returned: all would be provided. The clock had started ticking.

All that remained was to seal the undertaking with a formal invitation and acceptance, a civic process without which, I learned, no arrangements can be considered *official.* *"Eight[4] welldressers from Youlgrave are invited to visit Erbach as the guests of the Kreisstadt from 9th to 18th May for the purpose of dressing two wells ... to be the guests of the Hans von der Au Folk Group, who with certain of the townspeople would assist with the dressing."*

Meanwhile, back at the ranch, Margaret had agreed with Fred that the aim of deflecting Murphy's 1st Law (*anything that can go wrong will go wrong*) would be served if they both worked to the same screen design. Accordingly, Fred made detailed scale drawings of his Bank Top boards and passed them on for transmission. With their respective teams already picked and briefed, all that remained was to complete their designs and hope for the best. It was fingers-crossing time and, as we shall shortly see it failed to work.

On 23rd April, the Regierungspräsident in Darmstadt wrote

---

[4] For whatever reason, my own invitation come separately from the Bürgeméister.

to the Clerk of the County Council:

> *"An old idea growing out of our twinning activities appears to be near its realisation. During the time from 9th to 18th May two designers and six assistants from Youlgrave with some German helpers will dress two wells in the historical centre of Erbach in the Odenwald. A lot of planning and work from both sides has been necessary to overcome many difficulties, as far as the technical details of the dressing are concerned, and it is my hope that a successful realisation of this endeavour will again prove the far-reaching means of our twinning."*

Er... perhaps a little more responsibility than we had bargained for but amen to the hope.

So it came to pass that, on Saturday, 9th May, 1970, nine welldressing missionaries set out from Manchester airport with a clear purpose in mind and the comfort of knowing that all contingencies had been covered. We would spend the next day in a relaxed sort of way, getting to know everybody, finding out where everything was, perhaps picking a few flowers and checking on the workplace.Then on Monday we would make an early start at welldressing in earnest. At least, so we fondly imagined ...

We had forgotten Murphy.

... and alarms ... The officials of Erbach who met us with their cars at Frankfürt Airport were warmth and charm personified, but had they told us the bad news there and then I doubt we would have left the airport concourse. We were well down the Frankfurt to Heidelberg road – too late to turn tail – before we discovered that the wooden screens were still awaiting construction, pending confirmation of the measurements. Fred just had not been believed – or more accurately – the translation of Fred's specification had not been believed. Our friends in Erbach, with no first-hand experience of what to expect, suspected that imperial and metric had been garbled in trans-

109

mission, so they had waited to see! There was more bad news to come. The clay turned out to be useless. Our hosts, according to hearsay, ever anxious to anticipate problems, had adjudged the consignment they had been soaking for three months too plastic for our purpose and had added sand to help it set. *Set!*

So much for our casual Sunday! But for all that, I would not have been deprived of what was to follow.

While the rest of the party went scouting in the forest for moss and lichen, Fred stood over the head joiner for a good slice of Sunday. Like the rest of us (save for Jim) he spoke no German, but he did have a smattering of Italian picked up on active service. Confident in the belief cherished by all true Britons that *foreign* is a homogeneous condition that responds to a common vocabulary, he set to ensuring there should be *no b * * * *y mistakes this time*, using a cocktail of words and gestures that had me guessing – and I knew what he wanted. We could have ended up with a rocking horse, or worse. In fact, I thought we were in danger of getting nothing more than a flea in the ear since Fred had begun to encourage the joiner, as he thought, with a title, no doubt flattering in Italy, that had far-from-felicitous associations in Germany. I needn't have worried. It seems technician can talk to technician in any language or none and, while understanding may sometimes be slow to dawn, dawn it will in the fullness of time and they will part happily knowing there will be *no b * * * *y mistakes this time.*

As for the other problems, we might have fretted less that Sunday had we been aware of the trouble-shooting prowess we would encounter next morning in the person of Bürgermëister Werner Börchers..

My good friend Werner, as he came to be despite our having hardly a word in common, was (and, alas, the *was* is now mortal) what the Americans would call a *ball of fire*. As I sat with Jim and the designers in the *rathaus* that Monday morning, I knew we were listening to some very forceful man-management; we were also seeing a classic demonstration of anxiety-suppression, had we but known it, that was to become palpable only when subsequently banished. Before mid-morning, one of the potteries had been persuaded to surrender probably a day's production and we had our clay, albeit in powder form. As for the timberwork, two cabinet-class screens – the work of several weeks in Derbyshire – were produced in less than thirty-six hours; and to round off the list, Jim had a written requisition to take round to the town florist to compensate for any unforeseen shortfall in available blooms.

Meanwhile, Margaret had used Sunday to prepare a small, clay-filled tray to test the durability of the flowers we thought to use later in the week. It was now in the lap of the gods.

Heigh ho ... To work we went with a vengeance at mid-day on Tuesday, undaunted by dry boards and a day-and-a-half less to play with. At last we knew we would produce two well-dressings, come what may, and I think that by the end of the day, our hosts were experiencing a genuine belief that up to now they had been able only to simulate in our presence. Heads would not roll, after all, the honour of the town would be saved – and *Michelstadt could wind its municipal neck in.*

This may be the moment to mention the domestic arrangements. Fred's team – wife Dorothy, Jim Evans and wife Ivy – were comfortably installed in the Eck hotel, while the rest of us – two Margarets, Jim and Emmie comprising the other team – were at Zum Baren (The Bear). Each was an attractive, small vernacular hotel whose only drawback was the lack of time we had to enjoy it. The place that occupied most of our waking moments – quite a considerable proportion of which would have been spent sleeping in England – was, of course, the castle workplace. And this was something else! At ground level off the courtyard, part of the castle basement had been converted to a large garage that the Graf had graciously vacated to our needs for the week. It was a welldresser's dream-house – full of atmosphere, big enough to accommodate several cars and equipped with a floor to wash them and a door big enough to allow us to take the work outside into the courtyard during the day. It had only one drawback – well, I say *drawback* but it was really a source of much amusement: on the night-shift the lights were controlled by an automatic time-lapse switch that plunged us in darkness every few minutes. Out would go the lights, up would go the cry *"Jim, put another bob in the meter,"* and on would come the lights to reveal the per-plexed faces of our German helpers. Somebody explained the joke, though I fancy the smiles that followed were less an indi-cation of shared humour than a concession to English demen-tia.

Our resident workmates, who were either town officials and their wives or members of the Folk Group, learned quickly and worked assiduously, in particular the former who had fewer distractions of their own, so that in no time at all we were well up to schedule. A few steps up from the garage was a large tackroom where coffee and cakes were in constant sup-ply, but to which we only sparingly retired. I think we might have frequented it more often, especially when the Bürgermëister sent in somewhat stronger beverages, but Fred kept our noses to the grindstone, even when eventually he had to admit we had caught up. By Tuesday evening the Bürgermëister, seeing ample evidence of progress and proba-bly comprehending for the first time the likelihood of a suc-cessful and spectacular outcome, allowed a return to his natur-al exuberance, thereby measuring the anxiety that had hitherto suppressed it. Nothing would do but he should take us off for a treat. Fred would have none of it: we were there to dress wells and dress wells we would till we dropped. He spoke for us all, as it happened, and it was left to Jim to translate it into a suitably gracious refusal that would leave the invitation open.

By mid-morning on Thursday, even Fred had to concede that we were back on schedule. There are checks to the progress of a welldressing, dictated by the need to hold back the more delicate materials, with which even the most demanding designer must comply. We had earned a break. So that afternoon Herr Börchers took us to see the deer and wild pigs in the forest *Wildpark,* to stroll in the English garden and to whoop it up in the tea rooms. Jim claimed never to have laughed so much in his life and it is not hard to understand why. It was one of those rare occasions when everything seems right with the world, when spirits sparkle, camaraderie abounds and when differences of nationality and language evaporate in the warmth of mutual regard. It is on these occasions that laughter comes most readily to lips and minds...

So it was in good heart that we returned to Erbach and the night shift and in good heart we remained through the trouble-free days that remained.

Prosit ... It was around this time I was asked – a touch obliquely, I thought – when the screens would be completed. I said 11 p.m. next day (Friday) might not be too far off the mark and Margaret agreed. Fred, no doubt still traumatised by the recent slings and arrows, was not yet ready to tempt Providence with any such over-optimistic predictions. Who knew what dramas still lay in wait for us? The same question was repeated from time to time on Friday and the answer remained the same, except in one particular instance: Jim E., who during the week had developed the art of teasing the younger members of the Von der Au, most of whom it transpired had an adequate grasp of English, told one of them that the screens had to be ready for 9 p.m. because that was the time the transport would arrive to take them to be erected *in* Michelstadt. *Michestadt!* The shock was palpable and faces fell like dominoes. Rumours never travel so rapidly as when they are impelled by consternation.

As for the dressing itself, apart from the rather quaint experience of working throughout the day, progress from Tuesday was almost as routine and predictable as it would be at home. There were interruptions from time to time – visits from the Press and television, which Jim S. fielded with aplomb, and the odd crisis, such as when Emmie got floored by a boisterous folk-dancing *fraulein* and finished up in the *krankenhaus* with a minor fracture. The pottery clay was a winner, the natural materials were all we could have wished for and our home-grown assistants applied themselves very assiduously to their rapidly-acquired skill.

We had come to know them well by now in the enclave that enclosed us. Of the town and its people we saw little. We passed them in the street, courteous, industrious and much like ourselves – or how we would like to think of ourselves – people who seemed content and fulfilled with their lot. How strange to think such men had gone to die in the trenches in Flanders and Picardy, men whom our fathers – and we in our turn – had come to think of only as *The Enemy*. What did they think of us? When the town came to us, as discreetly and quietly it did, we were too intent on welldressing to socialise. What did they think of these English strangers who had come to work like gnomes in their castle? Only now, in realising that without it my story is incomplete, does it occur to me that I never knew what the average Erbacher made of us. The best I can do is to offer you an extract from the Darmstädter Echo dated Freitag, 15, Mai, 1970, for the translation of which I can claim no credit.

So, in the end, we were ready to finish at 11 p.m. on Friday (although Fred still needed to be convinced of the fact). The time had come to rear up the boards and inspect our handi-work, a task so routine and matter-of-fact to welldressers everywhere that we failed to notice that our hosts were hold-ing their collective breath. Unbeknown to us, the conviction had been growing among them throughout the week that, log-ically, the boards would be displayed horizontally – how else could the clay be kept in place? But courteous to the end, they concealed their anxiety and looked disaster *bravely* in the face when our intentions became plain, or at least, bravely by those who could bear to look at all. In the event, the German clay proved to have all the tenacity of our English equivalent, so their fears were as groundless as their relief was exuberant. It made no small contribution to the exhilaration that was to follow.

Throughout the late afternoon and into the evening there had been comings and goings centred on the tackroom, which the *Englanders* were discouraged from visiting and, when we eventually managed to drag Fred from his welldressing (he would have been titivating it all night), we learned the reason why. Before us lay a feast: linen-clad tables, food and wine in abundance and the Von der Au musicians, in all their finery and with their instruments to play for us. A little late for Youlgravians to be starting a party, perhaps, but it needed no warming up. In no time at all we were oompahing with the best of them and at one stage I seem to remember seeing Margaret on the table waving my walking stick, though what she was doing with it and how she got there I am still at a loss to know. Happily, she didn't have to follow Emmie into the *krankenhaus*.

And this, being about welldressing, is really the end of the story. But on the pretext that one good reason for sustaining and sharing ancient customs is the inevitable realisation that we all have more in common than we thought, perhaps I may be allowed to tell the sequel.

The two Jims and Fred (equal opportunities still not yet having penetrated Youlgrave's lifestyle) were up at 6-o-clock that morning as the ladies slept on. They were joined by able-bodied townsmen (the chaps were, that is!) in mounting and framing the screens on their dedicated sites. I should have been there to see it, an event that six months earlier had seemed as feasible as time travel, the culmination of much planning and preparation by people who would never see it. There it was, the triumph of hope over reality, and I was still abed. All I can offer in witness to this historic occasion is a laconic extract from Jim's journal:

> **Saturday:** *We went down at 6a.m. to fix up the Welldressings. What a job! The Germans were so meticulous.*

115

In Youlgrave we fix up the boards and hope for the best. Here they measure up to the last cm.

Whit Saturday morning, 16th May, was fine and bright – a little too bright for our bleary eyes – and the town was already thronged with visitors by the time the rest of us surfaced to inspect our handiwork. It passed muster. What came as a surprise to us was the way in which the Folk Group had dressed the remaining wells and it came, too, as something of a revelation. Saplings and foliage had been brought from the forest and artistically arranged as a bower at each well. Into the greenery had been woven garlands and paper flowers, so unusual to our unaccustomed eyes yet striking a chord in the deep recesses of memory.

I could not help but think this was how our own welldressing must have begun. The further back one looks at old pictures of Youlgrave welldressings the more the size and significance of the screen recedes and the more the garlanding predominates. It may have been romantic fantasy but it was, to me, clear evidence that the origins of welldressing lay in the pre-history before national divisions were established and when the aspirations of mankind found a simple and common expression. I doubt I was alone in this perception. There had developed a bond of fellowship between ourselves and our hosts that could not be dismissed as the result of a week's working companionship: the explanation must have lain in a more instinctive, arcane awareness.

There were big celebrations that Saturday. The town was bedecked, the streets were thronged with visitors from afar and V.I.Ps mingled with the merrymakers. I cannot think it was just to do with the welldressing – the occasion must have had some other significance, but if I ever knew, I have now forgotten what it was. There was (literally) dancing in the streets, mostly from the splendidly-performing Von der Au, and by the look of it the local *brauhaus* benefited considerably from the event. We, the welldressers were entertained in the

Festhalle that evening and there was much letting down of hair. I always think the English are never quite up to spontaneous merriment in mixed company; we tend to be wooden, lost for ideas when it comes to *doing our bit*. On this occasion honour was saved unwittingly by Fred and Dorothy, who took the floor to dance and suddenly found themselves alone, performing to an admiring audience. It should be said that ballroom dancing was (and still is) their favourite pastime and no doubt Fred's feet drew added panache from the thought of all those *gremlins* left foiled and defeated behind us. Whatever the inspiration, it served to demonstrate that dressing wells was not the sole item in our repertoire and spared the rest of us the strain of having to prove it.

At some time during the evening, the Bürgermeister announced the creation of a new post of *Brunnenschmücker-führer* to the Kreisstadt and I was appointed to be the first holder of the office – an honour indeed but, alas, also honorary.

Next day he took us sightseeing in Heidelberg. We stood on the castle walls to view the majestic sweep of the wooded hills into the Neckar valley and as we gazed down in awe over the ancient town and its university, we mused on the spell of the past and the custom that had brought us so far from home. Why is it we are drawn to the past, wherever we may happen to be, with a warmth undiminished by the chauvinism of the times we live in?

Auf Wiedersehen ... It was time to go home. Next day we packed our bags, our trophies and souvenirs, and said fond farewell to our hosts, leaving them in due course to demolish our handiwork before it crumbled. We learned only long afterwards that from Saturday onwards they had taken the precaution of posting an overnight watchman to ensure that this final act of demolition would not be performed prematurely by some crank or vandal, a precaution that had not featured in our original *list of things to do*. It was unthinkable to us at that time that anyone would maliciously damage a well-dressing, but sadly, our local experience in recent years has confirmed that such typical German thoroughness owed more to prudence than to pessimism.

That is not the end of the story. In 1974 the Hans von der Au Folk Group came to stay with families in Youlgrave and to perform to enthralled audiences throughout the County. Friendships that had been sustained over the four years past were renewed: new bonds were forged. It was a joyful time – a scrap-book occasion which I feel sure must have been the topic of even more correspondence between the Regierungspräsident and the Clerk of the County County *on the far-reaching means of our twinning*. With such memories are the passing years unspent...

There is a postscript. Ten years after the first excursion we were invited to return. 1980 was a special year for Erbach, to the celebrations of which we would add our welldressing embellishment. This time, both we and our hosts knew what to expect. Faces had changed on our side, the domestic arrangements had changed on theirs, but we all knew the form. It was lovely to be back, though I wonder if we weren't a trifle superfluous. They had learned well ten years before and could turn out an English well-dressing to match the best, as indeed they did. And as is only to be expected, they had used their native ingenuity to experiment in ways that we, inhibited by the traditional way of doing things, could hardly contemplate. At one site, instead of having the screen as a flat facade in front of the well, they had surrounded the stone tank that comprised it with a series of four boards, each of which depicted one of the four seasons. *Winter* was stunning. I had never before seen a snow-scene portrayed in a well-dressing and, come to think of it, I don't believe I have ever seen another. In the Holy Land of Youlgrave welldressing portrayal, the sky is always blue and the sun always beats down. Strange that, for on the only occasion I visited the Holy Land the snow lay three inches thick in Haifa.

Memories grow dim, so they say, and it's true enough, though the dimness is that of a turned down wick that can be so easily restored with the flick of a knob. Places and events come back as I write, together with the faces of all those who, in so short a time, became enduring friends – the Bürgermëister, Frau Hilde Fraas the leader of the Folk Group who bore her war-widowhood without resentment, and so many of their colleagues – the real people to whom we had been drawn through our common heritage. It would be too easy to get fanciful about the role of welldressing in the cause of peace and understanding; suffice it to say that international friendship and understanding derive from *mutual* regard for custom and tradition and make it that little more difficult for politicians to distract us.

If there seems less to remember about that second visit, it is I suppose because there was neither crisis nor deliverance to punctuate it. One thing I do remember clearly from the 24th May, 1980: although, again, the reason for the celebration escapes me, there was a V.I.P. luncheon to which we were all invited and at which the Regierungspräsident, with charming ceremony, presented me with an illuminated certificate promoting me to the rank of *Brunnenschmückeroberführer*. It hangs on the wall of my study and I can see it from where I sit.

Brunnenschmückeroberführer, indeed! Whoever would have thought it?

Extract from Darmstädter Echo, 17th May, 1970

ENGLISH WELLDRESSERS EMBELLISH ERBACH

Nine artists are at work in the town - Old Custom from the 14th Century

Nine English Welldressers from the little town of Youlgrave in the County of Derbyshire have been staying (as our reporter says) since the 9th of May in the town of Erbach to demonstrate for Whitsuntide their traditional art, which is very well known in England. The invitation to these artists was a result of the partnership between the County and the Regierungsprasident of Darmstadt.

During a visit to Erbach the Chairman of the County Council had learned of the Whitsuntide custom of decorating wells and offered to send the best well dressers in England to Erbach to give a demonst- ration of their art, which is totally differ- ent from the form prevailing in Odenwald. The journey to Erbach was made possible through the co-operation of the Minister for Economic Affairs and Agriculture of Hesse, the Regierungs- prasident and the European Council.

The town of Erbach has found accommodation for the nine artists within its walls and Count Franz of Erbach-Erbach placed the corridor of the tower in the castle at their disposal as a workshop. The nine welldressers, led by Chairman Norman Wilson, are being entertained by members of the Hans von der Au Goup, who are also helping them with their work.

In particular, certain flowers and other materials are needed at the Castle Tower in Erbach this Friday and the

inhabitants are asked to help obtain these. District Head Forester Karl Schmidt has also placed himself at the disposal of the welldressers and has already been able to obtain for them numerous necessary materials.

The best known custom - and certainly also the most beautiful - of the English County of Derbyshire is the so-called welldressing, the artistic decoration of the wells on particular public holidays. This custom, whose historical origin can be traced as far back as the 14th Century, has to do with the ancient rights of dedication of the life-giving wells. In the way this custom is carried out in Youlgrave, it represents a harmonious combination of artistic expression - very often of biblical motifs - and the most perfect craftsmanship. This art has been handed down for centuries from generation to generation in the little town of Youlgrave, which has 1500 inhabitants.

Wooden screens are covered with soft clay which has been prepared months in advance. The outlines of the design, which is a new one every year, are drawn into this clay and picked out in various materials. Small parts of flowers and blossom, moss, lichen and parts of fir cones are then inserted into the clay during days of minute and difficult work, until a mosaic-like and many-coloured picture emerges, which

becomes a point of attraction by the wells for days on end for numerous visitors from all parts of England.

The people of Youlgrave have always refused until now to decorate wells out- side their own village, but now these nine welldressers are proud of their invitation to Erbach. Deliberately only a few of them - but nevertheless providing their own tea - have come to Erbach so that it should not be possible without the assist- ance of their German friends to complete the work. Thus welldressing in Erbach becomes a symbol of friendly collabor- ation .

Tomorrow, Saturday at 6 a.m., the English team and their German helpers will carefully carry the completed works of art to the wells on the market place in Erbach and in the Städtel and set them up there. Since various of the materials - as for example the clay and the flowers - are not identical with those in England, we look forward to this moment with particular excitement. The official opening of the decorated wells will also take place tomorrow, Saturday, at 2.30 pm.

The wells which have been decorated by the Hans von der Au Group will be opened at the same time. Everybody is invited to the opening and to inspect the welldressings, and guests of honour from the State Government of Hesse and from the Regierungspräsidium are also expected

120

The Wildpark

Apparently deep in conversation with the author, the Bürgermëister leads the welldressing team through The English Garden on an afternoon's relaxation. It is an illusion – they have no common language, but welldressing seems to generate a language of its own. From left to right: Margaret F, Ivy, Jim S, Fred, Margaret G, Dorothy, Emmie, a host and Jim E (?). In the background is the country house of the Graf whose castle provided the welldressing workshop.

Well dressed for Manchester weather but hoping for better in Erbach. From left to right: Norman Wilson, Ivy Evans, Dorothy Shimwell, Margaret Gladwin, Jim Evans, Margaret Fell and Fred Shimwell. (Jim Shimwell was pointing the camera).

The Flight into Egypt

Margaret's labour-saving decision to recycle her 1969 picture (seen on the right) makes for an interesting comparison. Because the usual materials and team are not available to her, she employs strong colour contrasts for effect instead of the subtle tones and shades that are the feature of her Youlgrave screens. The border includes the German and British flags, the Hesse crest (barred leopard rampant) and the current Derbyshire coat of arms. Note the difference in board design, she and Fred agreed to use the same Bank Top shape to avoid complications.

THE FLIGHT INTO EGYPT

1969

Stilling the Storm

The devices in Fred's border complement Margaret's. The town crest of Erbach in the headboard is flanked by elephant heads to symbolise the ivory-carving fame of the town. The rams' heads in the supporters are, of course, the Derbyshire counterpart. Because of the early date many of the flowers were florist grown, hence the somewhat more exotic colours than are seen in a Youlgrave screen, but they lend themselves better to Fred's usual style than to Margaret's.

Erbach

1970

Stillung des Sturmes

Chapter 7

APOSTLES

Families ... Not so many years ago, when countryfolk were far less mobile than they are today, the same family names recurred like strands through the history of a village such as Youlgrave. Some surnames were not only a record of family relations, they were often an indication within a district of where the bearer lived. Some still flourish, but others that have endured for centuries are suddenly no longer to be found. Familiar names in Youlgrave, like Toft[1], Garratt and Coates are just a few of those that have declined from prominence to extinction in little more than a generation. Others will soon follow.

The continuity of surnames and occupations owes much to the fact that people's interests and aspirations did not stray far beyond the parish boundary and this self-containment – which we now call roots – invigorated the commercial and social life of the village. People rarely locked their doors. It was a neighbourhood then; now we have a Neighbourhood Watch.

---

[1] So much for the expectations of the good ladies of the village in their 1931 *Account of Youlgrave, Middleton and Alport: "Evidence of the occupation by the Danes is strong in our own village in the family names of* Toft ..." Sic Transit gloria Mundi.

I grew up with the impression that the world was populated by people called Evans, Birds, Oldfield and Shimwell, little realising that in the wider world the Wilsons lay a good deal thicker on the ground than any. The names were not only a village particular, they often pointed to the bearer's livelihood: the Oldfields, for instance, were mostly leadminers, the Birds' were associated with husbandry, while the name Evans would, as often as not, be the badge of a craftsmen. As for the Shimwells ...

Should some future anthropologist stumble on this connection between surname and occupation in pre-millennial Youlgrave, he will surely conclude that *Shim* is an ancient word for *keeper or high priest of*. Shimwells adorn the annals of welldressing as candles light up a Christmas tree. And Fred claims he can trace a relationship to all of them: he has more distant cousins than an intestate millionaire. Their influence is everywhere. It is almost impossible to tread the path of recent welldressing history without tripping over one or other of them. With Fred and Jim we are already acquainted; Bill and his son, David, have written the only factual welldressing record for Youlgrave; and that latter-day doyen of the tradition, Oliver, never ceased to be a Youlgrave man at heart. Wherever you look there is a Shimwell somewhere in the background.

It may come as a surprise to students of the art, not least in Tideswell and Wormhill, that I claim Oliver for Youlgrave. He, I'm sure, would not demur. He never lost his dedication to the village where he began his welldressing career – at his father's knee, so to speak – and his enduring affection for Youlgrave shone through the writing and television in which he featured. Sadly, thinking as we so vainly do that time and tide – and death – will await our convenience, I tarried too long with the chance to enhance these pages with his thoughts.

The Apostle ... However, latter-day doyen though he may have been, it was his father, Edwin, who must be accorded the man-

127

tle of St. Paul in spreading the gospel of welldressing . Teddy was a devout man, the church organist, for whom welldressing was an expression of his Christian faith. Had he been a doctor, say, instead of the schools attendance officer that he was, it is likely he would have applied his missionary zeal abroad in much the same way as he brought enlightenment to those less-discernibly in need of it at a local level. He was a remarkably dedicated – even fervent – exponent of the welldressing art, and, as his daughter Marion declares: *"in no place would he rest content until it had a welldressing."*[2]

Edwin was born of Youlgrave stock in 1873 and was not long past his majority before he was changing the face of welldressing in Youlgrave and, by extension, in the Peak District as a whole. He took charge at the Reading Room in 1895 and in the course of four of the next seven years he refined and remodelled the size and appearance of the screen. Instead of the more-or-less flat board, he produced a design that had depth and classical features. The recessed picture board was framed by pilasters supporting a transom set forward on corbels, above which a semi-circular headboard carried the text. It was an altogether bigger and more ambitious work of art than welldressers had hitherto aspired to and it marked a new sophistication in welldressing design. J.W. & D.W. Shimwell make the interesting observation that this very distinctive screen, still evident in other villages, marks the apostle's progress, so to speak, as Edwin and his family moved their places of abode from 1935 until his death in 1947.

There were also financial implications. It came as a surprise to learn from his daughter (now Mrs. Marion Allport) that Edwin was quite relaxed about the practice of paying the welldressers for their services. It seems at odds with his devout beliefs, but there may be more in this than meets the eye. His

---

[2] Welldressing ordered their lives. She was required as a matter of routine to monitor the flowers that were in the gardens she passed (and perhaps in the jardinieres she saw through the windows, too).

view, she explains, was that the men had to be compensated in those straitened times *for the unpaid time they had to take from work* and since the effect of his innovations was to increase their workload, it may have been expediency rather than liberalism that framed his judgment. Was it still a spare-time activity until Edwin came up with his king-size board? Well, we do know that, around this time, Youlgrave welldressers were being paid to dress wells in Buxton – whatever that may tell us.[3]

When Edwin and his family left Youlgrave to live in Stoney Middleton the latter instantly sported a welldressing. In similar succession, Stoney Middleton was followed by Tideswell and Wormhill and there is reason to believe that Eyam & *Litton benefited from a less intimate association. Where they chose to live was the place currently most in need of a welldressing custom* – is what I would like to report Mrs. Alport as having told me, but it would be stretching the truth. Anyway, I think that is what she meant to say.

The Acts ... It must be comparatively easy, nowadays, for someone of the skill of an Edwin Shimwell to set up a welldressing from scratch. People have leisure to spare, are generous with their time and money and their reward is assured in the crowds that will surely turn up to admire their handiwork. Unsurprising, therefore, that welldressing should have blossomed like its own stock in trade.

It was not so in 1935, nor for the 20 or so years that followed. It was a time during which the growth in welldressing activity owed much to the encouragement of the Youlgrave designers, who themselves, had to pick up the traces after the

---

[3] History repeated itself in 1990 when Youlgrave welldressers – and quite a few non-welldressers – were paid to produce a screen that was used to create a television advertisement for Buxton Water. It was not a success. The advertisers ignored advice that their illustration would not effectively transpose to a welldressing screen, They knew better.

rigours of war. A fairly comprehensive list of the villages that benefited is provided by J.W. & D.W. Shimwell (at Appendix II) but it does need to be emphasised that the enterprise was entirely provided by the designers as individuals and not by the Committee. The point is illustrated by the following extracts from the Minute Book:

17th May, 1949

This was a special meeting called to discuss the possibility of our helping the Ashford British Legion to dress several wells on the day of their Rally – Saturday, June 11th. Two represen-tatives were present from Ashford and they stated their requirements. It appears that it is twelve years since the Wells were dressed at Ashford, that there were no boards in existence and as far as the representatives knew there was no-one in Ashford capable of dressing the wells,[4] so they would require people from Youlgrave to go and supervise them ... what actu-ally was required was our men (sic) to go and do the whole job from start to finish, and the general feeling of the meeting was that in view of the fact that we were dressing our own wells only a fortnight later, this was impossible. After further dis-cussion, an offer was made to the representatives that if they were willing to dress their wells at a later date, say towards the end of July, we would do all we could to help them. This offer was accepted and they promised to communicate with us later and also send someone to watch us at work on our Wells.

18th July 1949

As nothing further had been heard from Ashford, it was pre-sumed that they had let the matter drop for this year.

And there the matter rested – or, at least, would have rested

---

[4] This reinforces my contention in Chapter 1 that the welldressing of 1829 could not have started from scratch.

but for a succinct explanation in a recent letter from Margaret: *"My parents and I went and worked alongside Ashford the first year they reinstated their welldressings."* Ashford will tell you there was a good deal more to it than that modest indication, but it does serve to illustrate the point: in welldressing, as in most else, enterprising individuals are likely to overcome problems that committees find insuperable. It must have been the time, or thereabouts, that Margaret had enough on her hands at home in starting up Coldwell again. Nothing daunted, she answered further calls from Pilsley and Etwall and embarked on her own lifelong mission of spreading the knowledge of welldressing by demonstrations and exhibitions too numerous to mention. It was not all devotion to welldressing: often her pet causes – the Womens's Institute and the Wesleyan church in particular – benefited from her unique brand of advertisement.

Meanwhile, Fred, too, was turning a helping hand. He helped to fly the flag at Chesterfield and Buxton, provided expert advice in the inauguration of Middleton-by-Youlgrave and Pleasley and has been designing Hartington since 1987.

From Edwin to Fred, the contribution of the Youlgrave line endures in festivals throughout the Peak. Less evident is the influence they have exerted over a much wider area through illustrated talks and lectures. Margaret is a recognised authority and much in demand. Ruth, as is to be expected, is a specialist in converting Salopian youth, talking to schools, organising trips to the Youlgrave festival from her Shropshire base and even coaxing the Salopians into their own annual festival.

Jim, it has to be said, is the true apostle in the international sense. The list of his initiatives, produced at my insistence, deserves to be quoted verbatim Here it is:

> •*Helped start Rowsley Welldressings* • *Helped with welldressing in Australia – advice, plans, materials – in the 1980's* • *Similarly helped at the Church of St. John, Manhattan.*

> •*Designed and dressed in Germany* • *Constructed demonstration welldressing and display that was used in South Derbyshire libraries for 15 months* • *Designed and led a team to construct demonstration at Hatfield House, Hertfordshire in 1982 and 1983.*
> •*Likewise in Derby Cathedral (1983)* • *Designed and led team to produce a television advert and* • *(this you will like – Ed) Supplied a demonstration for the National Institute of Funeral Directors.*

There is much more if only there were space to tell. Jim's comprehensive list of slides has introduced welldressing to scores of organisations most of whose members had never heard of Youlgrave let alone its custom. I know of no other designer, anywhere, who spent so many winter months travelling in response to requests from far and wide. How little his co-welldressers realised when they turned up for their annual duty what deeds had been performed in their absence.

There are others who have to be nameless: visitors who have come to admire, returned to help, to photograph and to spread the word in their homeland; visitors from overseas[5] who have found not just a quaint *olde worlde custom* but an inspiration – perhaps an echo of their own beliefs and folk-memories – and who share their experience with neighbours not as proud owners of holiday snaps but as apostles. Were it otherwise, I think the thousands of visitors who flock to welldressing throughout Derbyshire (and now on its fringes) would pay scant regard to the services of thanksgiving instead of thronging to the processions and congregations as they do.

We live in an age of mass communication and perhaps it is only a matter of time before these apostles are replaced by the Internet. What will happen when the whole world can learn about welldressing at the touch of a button?

---

[5] Margaret had a Danish lady who travelled from home every year to help at Coldwell and there are others.

We welldressers may feign indifference, as the old-timer remarked years ago: *We would keep dressing the Taps even if nobody came.* But, secretly, we love an audience and if technology should present us to the people of the world at large ...

.... we shall just have to hope they don't all come at once.

EPILOGUE

A book about welldressing has no tidy end any more than it has a discernible beginning. Too many questions remain unanswered, the most enigmatic of which is surely this: How can a custom so closely associated in observance and concept with a vanished past, endure in a society where, by all accounts, the notion of giving thanks for anything at all is likely to prove more bewildering than compelling? And yet it thrives.
  Why do we do it?

> **Fred:** *No choice ! once committed you are never allowed to go. Although it can be stressful and worrying for periods, I enjoy every minute.*

> **Margaret:** *For me the really important thing is not why I started but why I have gone on all these years. For one thing I just love and find enormous satisfaction in the actual tactile experience, the 'doing' but perhaps most of all I love working with the team – working with, not just alongside. There is something special about working with a group of friends who are not necessarily artistic in their own right, to create something as uniquely beautiful as a welldressing. Then, too, it's back to one's roots, is it not? I have tremendous pride in the standard of work we produce representing Youlgrave.*

134

Jim: *I do believe that Youlgrave Welldressings are a very special religious occasion and I trust we shall never allow them to become anything else. People are well-satisfied with the tranquility and sincerity of our well dressings and that is enough.*

APPENDIX 1

*The following summary was written by Mrs. Margaret Fell in 1985
and photocopied for the benefit of visitors:*

A WELLDRESSING IS COMPOSED ALMOST ENTIRELY OF LIV-
ING MATERIAL. IT IS CREATED ON A BED OF CLAY, THE MOIS-
TURE IN THE CLAY PRESERVES THE FRESHNESS OF THE
DRESSING.

STAGE 1 THE BASE OF THE DRESSING IS A SET OF BOARDS –
BEST DESCRIBED AS SHALLOW WOODEN TRAYS. FOR TWO
WEEKS THEY ARE SOAKED IN THE RIVER (DRY BOARDS
WOULD DRAW THE MOISTURE FROM THE CLAY)

THE BOARDS ARE DRESSED SEPARATELY, ONLY COMING
TOGETHER WHEN THE WORK IS COMPLETE AND READY TO
BE ERECTED.

THE CLAY IS PREPARED TO A SOFT, BUT NOT WET, CONSIS-
TENCY. IT IS LITERALLY FLUNG ONTO THE BOARDS - TO
EXPEL THE AIR AND TO HELP IT TO "KEY". IT IS THEN BEAT-
EN DOWN AND SMOOTHED OFF TO A DEPTH OF $1/2 - 3/4$
INCH.

STAGE 2 THE BOARDS ARE MOVED INDOORS AND SET UP AT
A CONVENIENT WORKING HEIGHT – ALLOWING SPACE TO
WORK ALL ROUND. BECAUSE THE MATERIALS TO BE USED
WILL DECAY IT IS ESSENTIAL TO "BRING ON" ALL THE
BOARDS AT THE SAME PACE.

THE DESIGNS HAVE BEEN DRAWN TO EXACT SIZE, THEY ARE

LAID, FACE UP, ON THE CLAY AND THE OUTLINES ARE PRICKED THROUGH AT REGULAR INTERVALS ... LEAVING THE DESIGN IMPRINTED ON THE CLAY IN A SERIES OF DOTS. THE OUTLINES ARE THEN MADE PERMANENT – MAIZE (HEN BEANS) AND THE SMALL BLACK CONES OF THE ALDER ARE TRADITIONALLY MUCH USED. THEY ARE CAREFULLY PUSHED A LITTLE WAY INTO THE CLAY – CONES CAN BE TOUCHING, GRAIN MUST BE ALLOWED A LITTLE SPACE TO SWELL, FOR FLOWING LINES AND CURVES THICK WOOL IS OFTEN USED.

STAGE 3 OUTLINING COMPLETE THE WORK MUST THEN PROGRESS ACCORDING TO THE KEEPING PROPERTIES OF THE MATERIALS TO BE USED – E.G. MOSS WILL NOT FADE, SO AREAS OF MOSS WILL BE WORKED FIRST (GREY LICHEN FROM THE GRITSTONE ROCKS, GOLDEN FROM THE LIME-STONE WALLS). IT IS SELECTED OR SHAPED TO FIT THE DESIGN, AND SIMPLY PRESSED LIGHTLY ON THE CLAY. THE REVERSE SIDE OFTHE GREY LICHEN IS USED FOR AREAS OF BLACK.

LEAVES BEING TOUGHER IN TEXTURE THAN PETALS ARE LONGER LASTING AND FOR THIS REASON ARE USED NEXT. FOR LEAVES AND PETALS THE TECHNIQUE IS THE SAME – ALWAYS STARTING AT THE BOTTOM, WORKING UPWARDS EACH LEAF OR PETAL IS PLACED INDIVIDUALLY IN POSTIION OVERLAPPING LIKE TILES ON A ROOF, OR SCALES ON A FISH, SO THAT IF IT RAINS THE RAIN WILL RUN OFF WITHOUT DIS-TURBING THE PETALS. BUTTERCUPS ARE THE ONLY FLOW-ERS USED WHOLE – THE HEAD IS NIPPED OFF LEAVING A SMALL STALK HELD AT AN ANGLE TO THE CLAY THE STALK IS "POKED" INTO THE CLAY AND THE HEAD FORCED UPRIGHT.

WELLDRESSERS ARE INGENIOUS IN FINDING MATERIALS TO REPRESENT PARTICULAR TEXTURES, EVEN "DEAD" MATERI-ALS ARE USED E.G. DRIED HYDRANGEA PETALS, DEAD DAF-FODIL LEAVES, STRAW, SEEDS AND GRASSES. ETC. FOR "PIC-TURES" FACES AND LIMBS ARE USUALLY MOULDED IN THE CLAY AND COLOURED WITH BRICKDUST, COCOA, ETC. SHEEPS WOOL AND ANIMAL HAIR ARE USED FOR BEARDS AND HAIR.

A DRESSING TAKES APPROXIMATELY A WEEK TO COMPLETE WITH A TEAM OF TWELVE OR SO WORKERS. THE DESIGNER IS IMPORTANT, HE OR SHE HAS A VISION OF WHAT THEY HOPE TO ACHIEVE – BUT! – NATURE IS IN CONTROL OF THE SEASONS. AVAILABILITY OF FLOWERS, THEIR COLOUR RANGE AND QUANTITY MAKES FLEXIBILITY ESSENTIAL. WELLDRESSING IS A TEAM TASK – NO ONE PERSON COULD UNDERTAKE SUCH A HUGE, PAINSTAKING PROJECT. IT DEMANDS A SHARING OF SKILLS AND COMMITMENT. ITS REWARDS ARE A SENSE OF ACHIEVEMENT AND THE SATISFACTION OF MUTUAL PARTICIPATION IN THE CREATION OF THIS UNIQUE FOLK ART OF WHICH DERBYSHIRE HAS SUCH A PROUD TRADITION.

MATERIALS (IN ORDER OF USE)
MOSS – grey and gold lichen
OUTLINING MATERIALS – maize, alder cone, spruce knobs, wool
LEAVES – variegated box
red berberis
silver weed
lambs ears

OTHER MATERIALS
rib
rhubard seed/dock seed

FLOWERS – buttercup (whole heads)
dog daisy
hydrangea
orange blossom
pyrethrum
viola/pansy
delphinium
cranes bill
red geranium

straw
sycamore stalks
dried hydrangea/daffodil
leaves
tree bark
cotton grass
honesty
sheeps wool
seeds

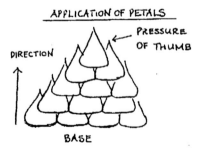

APPLICATION OF PETALS

PRESSURE OF THUMB

DIRECTION

BASE

APPENDIX II

The following account was written and published in 1974 by J.W. & D.W. Shimwell, who have kindly consented to the reproduction of this extract:

A History of Youlgrave Welldressing

The origins of the unusual Derbyshire custom of well-dressing are obscure and there have been many discussions on the subject. On the contrary, the methods used in the process are comparatively well known. Both these aspects are discussed in the comprehensive works of Crichton Porteous and to consider them further here would only lead to repetition. The history of the development of well-dressing, or, more correctly, tap-dressing in the village of Youlgrave is not well documented and an inspection of the available data indicates that the custom has had a chequered history and complex evolution

The Fountain was decorated at its erection in 1829 and folk-memory states that the custom continued for about twenty years before dying out. Searches of contemporary newspapers, however, have not provided corroborative evidence. When the second waterworks scheme was opened in July 1869 several of the newly erected taps were decorated and the Fountain had elaborate dressings on two sides. The east side consisted of a recessed board with two side panels The main picture was of a bible on a cushion and the side panels bore the crests of the Duke of Rutland and William Pole Thornhill. The south side decoration was a large spruce arch, divided into two smaller arches with boards bearing the crest of Miss Hannah Bowman and the monogram of T S Smith, the benefactors of the water schemes. The designer of the former was Henry Shimwell and of the latter, John Garratt.

For the next five or six years the taps were dressed in late July to coincide with the annual flower fete of Youlgrave Horticultural Society. Along with prizes for the heaviest root of celery and the two tallest hollyhocks the Society awarded two prizes of 30 shillings and one pound for the best tap dressings. In 1874, the first prize was awarded to William Shimwell for a design bearing the inscription "The Earth is the Lord's" at the base of a water ewer surrounded by doves and wreaths. Second prize went to Charles Wright for a decorative shield with an arch and garland festoon. The Horticultural Society stopped its sponsorship in 1875 and dressing was suspended until 1879 when the following notice appeared in the High Peak News of June 28th:

"We have great pleasure in stating that the once annual custom of welldressing will be revived at Youlgreave this year on Thursday next, the 3rd of July. All the arrangements are under the able superintendence of Mr Knowles and we sincerely hope it will be a great success".

It seems that it was not a success for there are no more reports of dressing until 1888, when two London gentlemen, Mr Horace Barry and Mr Bew who were visiting the annual Court Thorntree gathering of the Foresters at the Thornhill Arms expressed a desire "for the tapdressing as of yore". They sponsored the dressing of the Fountain tap by William Shimwell with the text "O ye wells, bless ye the Lord" in crimson and gold with the royal coat of arms above. In subsequent years, the Foresters paid the cost of dressing this tap and the custom became an integral part of their parade and court celebrations on the Wednesday nearest to Midsummer Day.

The first positive record of the dressing of the present five taps is from the year 1894. In order to encourage other designers, four ladies (including Miss Knowles and Mrs. Barry) established a fund to be divided in prizes. The Fountain dressing was considered to be too good for the competition and in this year Mr Shimwell excelled himself with a complex design of an old-fashioned water mill with a moving wheel. First prize of 25 shillings went to the Bank Top dressing of "Come ye to the waters" by Caroline Oldfield. The tradition of dressing for prizes continued until 1896 when a newspaper report bemoaned the fact that most of the benefactors of the fund had either left the district or died.

Queen Victoria's Jubilee year of 1897 was celebrated by extensive festivities which included the planting of the yew tree in the churchyard and two tap-dressings. William Shimwell as always designed the Fountain dressing in the form of Windsor Castle with "Victoria 1837-97" below, while Caroline and George William Oldfield dressed Bank Top tap. Between 1898 and 1900 only the Fountain tap was dressed and in 1901 a committee was set up to encourage dressing for competition The Reverend W Parker Stamper as treasurer collected subscriptions to a fund which allowed the donation of five prizes ranging from two pounds down to ten shillings. At this time the dressing moved to its present celebration date of the nearest Saturday to

Midsummer, or St John the Baptist's day if a religious calendar is consulted. It was in this period that religious "blessing of the wells" services were initiated. Apart from this feature, 1902 is noteworthy for the appearance of the first human figure on a tap-dressing when a likeness of King Edward VII in the form of a huge penny was executed by Charles Webster at Coldwell End.

In 1903, funds did not permit the dressing of more than two wells and the following year, the committee was reconstituted and was composed mainly of dressers. The vicar became chairman of this, the first Youlgrave Welldressing Committee Prizes were not offered but the collections in boxes situated in front of the wells were shared equally by the dressers. Between 1904 and 1910 five taps were dressed annually and a balance sheet for the latter year indicates that each group of dressers received two pounds. Only three wells were dressed in 1911, the year of the coronation of King George V. At the Reading Room, Samuel Nuttall portrayed a likeness of the King, at the Fountain, Edwin Shimwell designed the royal coat of arms, and at Bank Top, George William Oldfield, as patriotic as ever, drew a crown and cushion design with "Long live the King" beneath. In 1912, however, the custom was dwindling fast and only Mr. Nuttall's team produced a dressing.

At both of the colossal parades of 1919 there were welldressings. In June, Edwin Shimwell decorated the Fountain tap with a picture of Brittannia and the text "Guide our feet in the way of peace" to coincide with the servicemen's Welcome Home Parade and Dinner. To celebrate its fiftieth anniversary the Water Committee sponsored the second dressing of all five taps in September, and this custom continued until 1927. The dressers were paid by the committee and collections taken at the parade went into the Waterworks funds. After a particularly wet year, the Water Committee withdrew their sponsorship and had it not been for the energy of Mr George W. Gimber, the schoolmaster, the custom might have faltered. He designed all five wells in 1928 and reformed Youlgrave Well-dressing Committee yet again. The enthusiasm returned and in the Waterworks centenary year all five wells were dressed twice.

The late twenties were noteworthy for changes in design. Before 1924 full length human figures were seldom depicted and architectural subjects were preferred. In 1929, six of the ten dressings incorporated figures and by 1933 all five taps depicted biblical scenes. Not all the designs were successful and several still remain notorious. From 1927, a portrayal of St Benedict with the caption "Saints are lovely in His sight" is well-remembered. At the time, a well-known village character was heard to comment – "Ay is a rum lookin chap; wimmin's frittened on im – thee darena goo un fetch th'watter from th'tap". The Bank Top tap was always dressed in the outbuildings of the Farmyard Inn and their second 1929 design was planned to show Jesus walking on the water. On the Friday night, the dressers from the Reading

Room had finished early and descended on the Farmyard seeking refreshment. The Bank Top company joined them and soon there were more bottles around the boards than flowers. Only a few men carried on dressing and next morning Jesus seemed decidedly waterlogged!

At the Coldwell End tap, Roland Shimwell seemed to produce controversial pictures each year as new avenues in design were explored. His 1934 design of the Crucifixion was the first attempt at the subject and his 1936 portrayal of Delilah as a voluptuous, semi-nude call-girl swelled the contributions to the collecting box. One of Youlgrave's best ever dressings was to be seen at Coldwell End in 1939. It was a picture of the head of Christ, based on a painting by the Italian artist, Guido. The intricate design was highlighted by the simple and effective border design of Clifford Roper whose caption "Father forgive them, they know not what they do" was particularly appropriate to the year.

From 1930 to 1939, the affairs of the dressers were directed by a committee of twelve, comprising three representatives from the two larger dressings at the Reading Room and Fountain and two from each of the others. In 1932, the religious service was recommenced and it has continued ever since. A house-to-house collection was undertaken and each tap had its own collecting boxes. Because the Reading Room and Fountain dressings were larger, they received half of the collection proceeds, while the other three shared the remainder. The tap-dressings were looked upon as an event which could provide an additional source of spending money, and as each tap kept the proceeds of its own collecting box the utmost care was taken to produce attractive designs. The committee clearly took the matter seriously for in 1931 it took steps to stop children from making their own well-dressings and in 1933 when the GPO were looking for a site for a telephone box, the committee objected to its erection "on any site likely to interfere with well-dressings".

The first charity tap-dressings were undertaken in 1940 and 1945 when only the Fountain tap was dressed and the proceeds were given to the Soldier's Comforts Fund and Welcome Home Fund respectively. All dressing was suspended between 1941 and 1944 but through the enthusiasm of William Boardman and Harold Lees the Welldressing committee was reformed in 1946. A fund was inaugurated and the names of dressers were entered in a register so that men could be paid one pound, women ten shillings, and juniors two shillings and sixpence from the proceeds of public collection boxes. In 1946, the Reading Room and Fountain wells were dressed and in 1947, 21 men, 10 women and 12 juniors took part in the dressing of these two taps and the Main Street tap. An account of the methods of dressing and the Youlgrave ceremony was broadcast by the North Regional BBC and after the dressers had been paid, the balance of the proceeds was

142

donated to the Peace Celebration Committee for the purchase of commemorative mugs.

Four wells were dressed in 1949 and the Main Street tap was moved to its present "Holywell" site The following year, Coldwell End tap became the fifth to be dressed. This year also saw the first proposal that dressing should be voluntary, but it was defeated, mainly because of fears that the custom would lapse. In 1956, however, it was unanimously agreed that all dressing should be voluntary and that the greater proportion of the proceeds should go to a single charity each year. Through these efforts, Cancer Research received £100 in 1956 and subsequent years the Guide Dogs for the Blind, R.N.L.I. and Red Cross all received well over £100

The strong tradition of well-dressing in Youlgrave in the twentieth century has had a marked effect on the revival and style of the custom throughout Derbyshire. Advice by Youlgrave dressers was given at Ashford, Marsh Lane, Pilsley and Etwall and Oliver Shimwell has developed the custom in Stoney Middleton, Tideswell and Wormhill and given advice at Eyam and Litton. Mr Shimwell and his team have also dressed the Tideswell boards in London, Manchester and Sheffield and a team from Youlgrave took the craft to Erbach, near Darmstadt in Germany in 1970. Prior to the dressing of the two wells in Germany, Margaret Fell and Fred Shimwell sent over the board specifications and details of the type of clay required. On arrival, the team discovered that nothing had been done and the German officials could not believe that such elaborate base boards were required for what to them was a simple ceremony. Eventually all the problems were resolved and the two dressings were a great success.

In the foregoing account of well-dressing in Youlgrave continuous reference has been made to the designers of the dressings because it is this group of people which has been responsible for changes and evolution in the custom. A comprehensive list of designers from 1894 is provided. These people are, however, only a single 'cog' in the welldressing 'machine' and in closing, mention must be made of the innumerable flowergatherers and dressers without whose energy the custom would have long since died.

Designers of Youlgrave Well-dressings since 1894
READING ROOM: 1894 Marsden Brothers; 1895-96 Edwin Shimwell; 1897-1900 No Dressing: 1901-02 Edwin Shimwell; 1903 Mr. Wattison of Wirksworth; 1904-14 Samuel Nuttall. 1915-18 No dressing; 1919-21 G.H. Ollerenshaw; 1922 George W. Gimber; 1923 G.H. Ollerenshaw; 1924-30 G.W. Gimber; 1931-39 Harold Lees; 1940-45 No dressing; 1946-55 H. Lees; 1956 H. Lees and N. Mercer; 1957-70 Nicholas Mercer; 1971-72 N.and R. Mercer; 1973 Ruth Mercer.

FOUNTAIN: 1888-1901 William Shimwell senior; 1902 William Shimwell junior; 1903-04 Edwin Shimwell; 1905 Miss Lee and Rev. W.P. Stamper; 1906-11 Edwin Shimwell; 1912 No dressing; 1913-14 Edwin Shimwell; 1915-18 No dressing; 1919-27 Edwin Shimwell; 1928 G.W. Gimber; 1929-34 Edwin Shimwell; 1935-36 Edwin and Oliver Shimwell; 1937-39 William Clark; 1940 W. Clark and F. Billinge; 1941-44 No dressing; 1945-52 William Clark; 1953 R. Bacon and F. Shimwell; 1954 W. Clark; 1955-70 David Dysor,; 1971 James Connolly.

MAIN STREET (1894-1947)/HOLYWELL LANE: 1894-96 F. Evans & J. Shimwell; 1897-1900 No dressing; 1901-02 G.H. Ollerenshaw & J. Shimwell; 1903 No dressing; 1904-05 G.H. Ollerenshaw; 1906-10 J.H. Shimwell; 1911-13 No dressing; 1914 J.H. Shimwell; 1915-18 No dressing; 1919? J.H. Shimwell; 1920-22 No dressing; 1923 Oliver Shimwell; 1924 Fred Billinge; 1925-26 No dressing; 1927 G.W. Gimber and H.Shimwell; 1928 G.W. Gimber; 1929-32 Harold Shimwell; 1933 Cecil Evans; 1934 W.Clark; 1935-39 Fred Billinge; 1940-46 No dressing; 1947 Ronald Bacon; 1948-63 R.Bacon and F. Billinge; 1964-1970 Fred Billinge; 1971 James Shimwell. ~

BANK TOP: 1894-96 Caroline Oldfield; 1897 Caroline and George William Oldfield; 1898-1900 No dressing; 1901-02 George E. Frost; 1903 No dressing; 1904-10 George E. Frost: 1911 George E. Frost and George W. Oldfield; 1912-18 No dressing; 1919-1922 Edmund Beebe; 1923-25 William Yates; 1926 W. Yates and E. Beebe; 1927 W. Yates 1928 G.W. Gimber; 1929 (i) Albert Oldfield; 1929 (ii}34 W. Yates; 1935 A. Tranter; 1936 No dressing; 1937 H. Lees; 1938 R. Bacon and Leonard Frost; 1939 R. Bacon; 1940-48 No dressing; 1949 M. Boardman and F. Shimwell; 1950 Fred Shimwell.

COLDWELL END: 1894 Jonathan Beebe and Charles Wright; 1895-96 Charlotte Needham; 1898-1900 No dressing; 1901-02 Charles Webster: 1903 No dressing; 1904-05 Jonathan Beebe; 1906-10 G.H. Ollerenshaw; 1911-1918 No dressing; 1919-25 Clifford Roper; 1926 A. Brassington and H. Shimwell; 1927 C. Roper; 1928-30 G.W. Gimber; 1931-39 Clifford Roper and Roland Shimwell; 1940-49 No dressing; 1950 Margaret Fell (nee Boardman).